Favourite Lessons

We Learned at School

The editor and publishers acknowledge with gratitude the cooperation of the Educational Company of Ireland in making available material from old school books.

First published in 1998 by
Mercier Press
5 French Church Street Cork
Tel: (021) 275040; Fax: (021) 274969
e.mail: books@mercier.ie
16 Hume Street Dublin 2
Tel: (01) 661 5299; Fax: (01) 661 8583
e.mail: books@marino.ie

Trade enquiries to CMD Distribution
55A Spruce Avenue
Stillorgan Industrial Park
Blackrock County Dublin
Tel: (01) 294 2556; Fax: (01) 294 2564

© Introduction Thomas F. Walsh 1998
© Extracts from school books
as specified in acknowledgements

ISBN 1 85635 240 4

10 9 8 7 6 5 4 3 2 1

Cover design by
Penhouse Design Group
Printed in Ireland by BetaPrint,
Newtown Industrial Estate,
Clonshaugh, Dublin 11

A CIP record for this title is available
from the British Library

FAVOURITE LESSONS
WE LEARNED AT SCHOOL

THOMAS F. WALSH

MERCIER PRESS

CONTENTS

Introduction

There was a time when children called their school books *lesson books* and when they never had any more than three or four books in their *satchel* on their way to school each morning. There was an Irish book, an English book, and a Catechism, and maybe a *New Progress Arithmetic*; anything else was a luxury. The teacher brought History to life with stirring tales about The Wild Geese or Eoghan Rua O'Neill. When Geography-time came he unrolled the big map of Ireland and we rattled off the counties of Connacht or took the perilous individual journey to the top of the class and pointed out where we thought the Knockmealdown Mountains were.

It is a fascinating thing to pore over those school books of yesteryear. They remind us of our own childhood and that of the generations that went before us. I loved finding the books from which I learned my lessons and I remember the joy I felt when I came across a book that my mother would certainly have used in school. It was an old brown-paper-covered copy of *The Fifth Reading Book* published for the Commissioners of National Education by Browne and Nolan of Nassau street in 1915. I recognised the lessons and poems she was fond of quoting, and from its fragile, yellowed pages her childhood unfolded to me like a pressed flower coming to life again. It felt somehow sacred.

Our old school books are, in themselves, a social history of our country. It is easy to see that there was an emphasis on right and wrong, on honesty and honest labour and a shunning of materialism and wealth. The world they represent was the Ireland of De Valera, a timeless place where people were supposed to be happy and content. It was an ideal world of childhood where we revelled in the legends of the old Celtic warriors like Fionn Mac Cumhaill and gloried in the stirring stories of our history, from Brian Boru to the Rising of 1916 – when History came to an abrupt end.

There was a certainty about everything, including right and wrong. We knew what was forbidden and what was commanded, and we knew what bad thoughts were. The price of eggs did not change much from year to year, so there was no need to change the arithmetic book. There were acres, roods and perches and pounds, shillings and pence; who ever heard of decimal currency? We knew that the towns where sugar was manufactured were Carlow, Mallow, Thurles and Tuam. It never occurred to us that sugar factories would ever close.

The Irish language took pride of place in our schools and in our school books. There are plenty of people who can quote the first page of Padraig Pearse's *Iosagán* by heart, and the opening lines of 'O Labhair an Teanga Ghaeilge Liom' are known to practically everybody of my generation.

The pervasive mood of these pages from our past is innocence, apparent in those pithy proverbs from the marvellous Vere Foster headline copies, which exhorted us to be wise and good. The songs and poems you find here are simple, honest and unadorned. The sample essays from the books of composition and grammar are about going to the bog to cut the turf or visiting the forge to see the blacksmith at work.

In the course of my research for the *Favourite Poems We Learned at School* it occurred to me that many people would love to see again the gentle lessons and beautiful illustrations from the school books of long ago that they thought were lost and gone for ever. Here, then, is a chance to have a peep inside the covers of your own childhood and perhaps awaken, for a fleeting moment, that lost innocence.

Special thanks to Frank Fahy and Brendan Tallon of The Educational Company.

Thomas F. Walsh
September 1998

ACKNOWLEDGEMENTS

p. 11: 'A Child's Morning Prayer' from *The Irish World Readers* Preparatory (Browne & Nolan); p. 12: 'It Belongs to Me' from *Land of Youth Readers* Introductory (The Educational Company); pp. 13–15: 'Jamie Watt and his Grandmother's Kettle' from *Reading Time* Preparatory (The Educational Company); pp. 16–17: Handwriting from *O'Curry Series of Irish Copybooks* (The Educational Company); pp. 18–19: Exercise from *The Model Arithmetic IV* (Browne & Nolan); pp. 20-25: 'The Island of Saints & Scholars' from *A Primary History of Ireland* (Longmans, Browne & Nolan); pp. 26–8: 'The Forge' from *Composition and Grammar* (Longman, Browne & Nolan); p. 29: 'Crann' from *Tír na Seod* (Brún agus Ó Nualláin); pp. 30–1: 'What Will Christ Say?" from *A Catechism of Catholic Doctrine* (Archdiocese of Dublin); pp. 32-7: 'Counties and Towns' from *An Outline Geography* (The Educational Company); pp. 38–42: 'A Story of Saint Brigid' from *Land of Youth Readers* Beginners (The Educational Company); pp. 44–5: 'Little Rules for Health & Happiness' from *Irish Countryside Readers* Junior (Browne & Nolan); p. 46: 'The Shadow People' from *Land of Youth Readers* (The Educational Company); pp. 47–50: 'Dublin Airport from *Land of Youth Readers* Senior (The Educational Company); pp. 51-3: 'Which Was the Stronger?' from *The Irish World Readers* Preparatory (Browne & Nolan); p. 54: 'Poem' from *On Wings of Words* Beginners (Browne & Nolan); pp. 55–7: Exercise 40 from *The Model Arithmetic VI* (Browne & Nolan); pp. 58–9: 'The Creed' from *Catechism of Catholic Doctrine*; pp. 60-3: 'The Old Man and His Ass' from *The Oriel Readers* (Browne & Nolan); p. 64: 'The Robin's Song' from *Day by Day* Preparatory (The Educational Company); p. 65: 'How Should We Pray?' from *Irish World Readers* Beginners (Browne & Nolan); p. 66: 'The Night Sky' from *Day by Day* Beginners (The Educational Company); p. 67: 'The Robin and the Pussy Cat' from *Irish World Readers* Preparatory (Browne & Nolan); p. 68: 'We had Tea' from *My First Book* (Browne & Nolan); p. 69: 'We had a Ride' from *My First Book* (Browne & Nolan); p. 70: A Riddle from *Land of Youth Readers* Introductory (The Educational Company); p. 71: 'Hot Cross Buns' from *Young Ireland Reader* Beginners (Browne & Nolan); pp. 72–3: 'Úlla agus Milseáin' from *Tír na nÓg* (Brún agus Ó Nualláin); p. 74: 'You Can't Please Everyone' from *Land of Youth Readers* Preparatory (The Educational Company); p. 75: 'Buttercup Gold' from *Irish World Readers* Preparatory (Browne & Nolan); pp. 76–7: 'In Town' from *Young Ireland Reader* Introductory (Browne & Nolan); p. 79: 'The Tinker Man' from *Young Ireland Reader* Introductory (Browne & Nolan) p. 78: The Seasons' from *Irish World Readers* Preparatory (Browne & Nolan); p. 80–2: 'The Balloon Man' from *Irish World Readers* Preparatory (Browne & Nolan); p. 83: 'Suas' from *Tír na nÓg* (Brún agus Ó Nualláin); pp. 84–5: from *Learn to Write* (The Educational Company); pp. 86–7: 'Courtesy and Politeness' from *Fifth Reading Book* (Browne & Nolan); 88–9: 'The Two Hughs' from *A Primary History of Ireland* (Longman's, Browne and Nolan); pp. 91–3: Shop Bills from *The Model Arithmetic IV* (Browne & Nolan); pp. 94-7: Latin and Greek Roots from *Fifth Reading Book* (Browne & Nolan); p. 98: 'The Little Lord Jesus' from *Day By Day* Preparatory (The Educational Company); p. 99: 'The Piper Charms the Rats' from *On Wings of Words* Intermediate (Browne & Nolan); pp. 100–101: Unitary Method II from *The Model Arithmetic V* (Brown & Nolan); pp. 102–3: 'My Birth-day' from *Fifth Reading Book* (Browne & Nolan); pp. 104–5: 'Íosagán' from *Ó Pheann an Phiarsaigh* (An Chomhlacht Oideachais); p. 106: 'On the Lee' from *Irish World Readers* Beginners (Browne & Nolan); pp. 107-9: 'A Day on the Bog' from *Composition and Grammar* (Longman, Browne & Nolan); pp. 110-12: 'Belling the Cat' from *Day By Day* Preparatory (The Educational Company); p. 113: Loop Joins from *Learn to Write* (The Educational Company); pp. 114-17: 'Cromwell' from *A Primary History of Ireland* (Longman, Browne & Nolan); pp. 118–9: 'The Wind From the West' from *Land of Youth Readers* Preparatory (The Educational Company); 120–1: 'Lines Addressed to a Seagull' from *Fifth Reading Book* (Browne & Nolan); pp. 122-27: The 4th, 5th and 6th Commandments from *A Catechism of Catholic Doctrine*; pp. 128–9: 'The Norsemen' from ; p. 130: 'An Firín Sa Ghleann' from *Tír na Seod* (Brún agus Ó Nualláin); pp. 131-5: 'History of the Old Testament' from *The Junior Bible History* (Browne & Nolan); p. 136-7: 'A Visit From the Sea' from *Day By Day* Preparatory (The Educational Company); p. 139-43: 'How Hans Saved Harlem' from *Land of Youth Readers* Preparatory (The Educational Company); p. 144: 'A Child's Evening Prayer' from *Irish World Readers* Preparatory (Browne & Nolan).

A CHILD'S MORNING PRAYER.

I thank Thee, Lord, for quiet rest,
  And for Thy care of me;
Oh! let me through this day be blest,
  And kept from harm by Thee.

Oh! let me love Thee, kind Thou art
  To children such as I;
Give me a gentle, holy heart,
  Be Thou my friend on high.

Help me to please my parents dear,
  And do whate'er they tell;
Bless all my friends, both far and near,
  And keep them safe and well.

Mary L. Duncan.

IT BELONGS TO ME

I like to look
At a nice new book,
As nice, as nice can be;
I like to look
At a nice new book,
And know it belongs to me.

JAMIE WATT AND HIS GRANDMOTHER'S KETTLE

Jamie Watt was a little boy who lived in Scotland many years ago.

One day, as he sat in his grandmother's kitchen, he saw clouds of white steam coming from the big black kettle that hung over the turf fire. Then the lid of the kettle began to bounce up and down.

" O Grannie! " he cried. " Something is making the lid of the kettle bounce up and down."

His grandmother laughed at him.

"That is only the steam," she said. "Did you think there was a giant in the kettle?"

Jamie said nothing. But even then a dream was forming in his mind.

Next day, Jamie sat again at the turf fire, and watched the lid. of the kettle bounce up and down.

"Grannie," he said, "if steam from the water in the kettle can lift the lid, why could not the steam from a great deal more water lift heavy weights and turn great wheels?"

"You are a dreamer, Jamie," said the grandmother. "Run and play."

But Jamie never forgot the giant in his grandmother's kettle. He wanted to set it to work and make use of its great strength.

People laughed at him.

"Poor foolish Jamie Watt is trying to harness the steam that comes from his grandmother's kettle," they said.

"He wants to make a steam engine that can lift weights and turn wheels."

But Jamie kept working away. He built steam engine after steam engine, but they were all failures.

At last, after many years, he built a steam engine that was not a failure. And you may be sure that nobody laughed at him then.

Steam does much of man's work to-day. It drives trains, it brings great ships across the sea, it turns factory wheels.

Jamie Watt saw his dream come true. He set a giant to work, and made use of its great strength. And it all began on the day when he sat in his grandmother's kitchen and watched the lid of the kettle bounce up and down.

Máṡ ꜰuaṙ an teaċṫaiṙe iṫ ꜰuaṙ an ꝼṙeaġṙa

If the messenger is cold so is the answer

Is minic do baın ouıne ɼlaᴄ ċum a bualaᴅ ꝼéın

One often cut a rod to chastise himself

EXERCISE

The following record was kept by a Dublin housewife who had 12 hens :

1949–50	Eggs	Shop Prices per doz.		Value of Eggs £ s. d.			Cost of Food £ s. d.		
		s.	d.	£	s.	d.	£	s.	d.
Nov.	192	5	6		?			19	0
Dec.	?	5	6	5	0	4½		19	4
Jan.	?	4	0	3	13	8	1	3	1
Feb.	178	3	6		?		1	1	8
Mar.	?	3	6	3	16	5	1	5	4
April	279	3	6		?		1	1	8
Total	?				?			?	

(1) Work out the value of the eggs at shop prices for November, February and April.

(2) Find the missing numbers of eggs for December, January and March.

(3) Find the total value of the eggs for the six months.

(4) Find the total cost of the food for the six months.

The total figures for the previous six months, May to October, were : Eggs, **854.** Value of eggs at shop prices, £13 7s. Cost of food, £4 8s. 8d.

(5) What was the total number of eggs for the year ?

(6) What was the average number of eggs per month ? (Divide the total for the year by **12.**)

(7) Find the cost of food per hen for the year.

(8) Find the value of eggs per hen for the year.

(9) Allowing for the cost of food only, find the profit per hen for the year.

(10) In an egg-laying test, **6** hens laid a total of **1,444** eggs in **46** weeks.

> (*a*) Find, as near as you can, how many eggs the **6** hens laid, per week.
>
> (*b*) Find the value of the total number of eggs at 2½d. each.
>
> (*c*) The cost of food was given as **19**s. 9d. per bird. Find the total cost of feeding the **6** hens.
>
> (*d*) By how much did the value of the eggs exceed the cost of feeding ?
>
> (*e*) Of all the eggs only **79** were not first grade. How many first-grade eggs did the hens lay ?

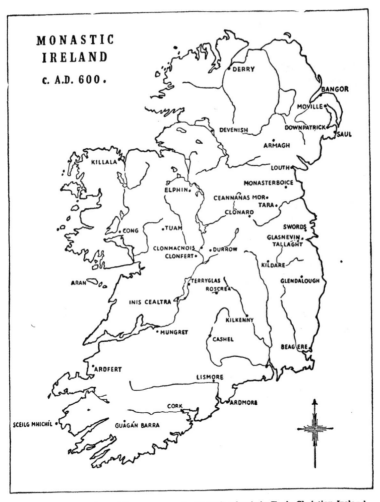

MONASTIC IRELAND c. A.D. 600.

DERRY
BANGOR
MOVILLE
DEVENISH
DOWNPATRICK
SAUL
ARMAGH
KILLALA
LOUTH
MONASTERBOICE
ELPHIN
CEANNANAS MOR
TARA
CLONARD
CONG
TUAM
SWORDS
GLASNEVIN
TALLAGHT
CLONMACNOIS
CLONFERT
DURROW
KILDARE
ARAN
TERRYGLAS
GLENDALOUGH
ROSCREA
INIS CEALTRA
KILKENNY
MUNGRET
CASHEL
BEAG ERE
ARDFERT
LISMORE
CORK
ARDMORE
SCEILG MHICHÍL
GUAGÁN BARRA

Map showing the sites of famous monasteries and schools in Early Christian Ireland.

20

The Island of Saints and Scholars

After the death of St. Patrick his work was carried on by other good men. By the year 500, most of the people of Ireland had become Christians.

Churches and monasteries

Churches and monasteries were built in every part of the country. The monasteries were not great stone buildings, like the monasteries of today. They were groups of small huts.

The huts were made of wood, or of mud and wattles; but in the west, where wood was scarce and stones were plentiful, they were made of stone. The wooden huts have long since crumbled away, but some of the stone huts may still be seen.

Each monk had his own little hut, usually built by himself, and there he slept on the bare ground or on a heap of straw.

As more and more huts were built, the place came to look like a village or small town. Each village had its little church, an eating-house, a library, and a guest-house where travellers could stay free of charge. There was also a mill where corn was ground to make meal for bread.

Round towers

A strong bank of clay and stones was made all round the village to keep out the wild animals.

Later on, round towers were built as belfries and watch-towers, and as places of refuge for the monks in time of war. They also served as store-houses and places of safety for books and for the beautiful things the monks made of gold and precious stones.

The islands

In those days, many holy men went to live on islands where they spent their lives in prayer and fasting.

Sceilg Mhichíl, a group of stone cells of a seventh-century island monastery off the coast of Kerry.

Books and writing

With Christianity came hand-written books. (There were no printed books until hundreds of years later). The monks made copies of the Bible and other good books, and taught their pupils how to read them.

In every monastery there were men, called *scribes*, who spent their time making copies of books.

Some of these old books are very beautiful. One of the finest is the Book of Kells. This is a copy of the Four Gospels in Latin, with beautiful ornamental capital letters and drawings painted in bright colours. This lovely book may be seen in Trinity College, Dublin.

Schools

Many boys and young men, and even old men, came, not only from Ireland, but from Britain and other countries, to study with the monks.

The pupils, like the monks, lived in little huts, and, except in bad weather, classes were held in the open air.

The pupils were taught Irish, Latin, music, drawing and the study of the stars. They wrote with pointed pieces of metal on strips of wood covered with beeswax. Their books were written with quill pens on vellum, which is a kind of stout paper made from the skins of goats, sheep and calves.

The Ardagh Chalice.

Metal work

The Irish metal-workers of those days were famous : they made many beautiful things of gold, silver and bronze. Among our most precious national treasures are the Ardagh Chalice and the Tara Brooch, which were made in the eighth century. These and other beautiful things may be seen in the National Museum.

Celtic crosses

The high Celtic stone crosses are also remarkable. Some of these are twenty feet tall, and many of them are beautifully carved. Among the finest are those at Monasterboice in Louth, and at Ceannanas Mór and Durrow.

The work of the monks

The monks did much useful work. They cut down the trees and cleared and drained the land, thus turning waste and marshy land into good grain-growing soil. They made copies of books and helped to spread knowledge of reading and writing. They cared for the sick. They were farmers, teachers, millers, weavers, tailors, artists, metalworkers and scribes.

High Cross of Muiredach, Abbot of Monasterboice, Co. Louth (died A.D. 923.)

For hundreds of years the Irish monasteries were centres of prayer, learning and activity. The fame of Ireland's holy and learned men spread abroad and won for our country its proud title of "The Island of Saints and Scholars."

This brilliant period in our history is known as Ireland's Golden Age.

THINGS TO DO

1. Look at the picture of the old stone cells on page 30. Tell what you notice about them.

2. If there is a round tower or a Celtic cross in your district, find out all you can about it.

3. Name some differences between your school and an old Irish monastic school.

4. Pretend you are a pupil at an old Irish school. Tell how you spend the day there.

5. If you live in or near Dublin, go to see the beautiful hand-written books in Trinity College. Write a little account of them.

6. Visit the National Museum, if you can. Look well at the Ardagh Chalice, the Tara Brooch and the other precious and lovely things in the Golden Age Section of the Museum. Tell your teacher all about them.

7. Make a little list of places where there were great monasteries and schools in Ireland of old.

II   A. Read this: then answer the questions:

THE FORGE

Our blacksmith, Patrick Murphy, is a friendly man, and the neighbours like to sit in his forge on winter evenings. Sometimes they talk ; but when the smith is busy, they sit and look on in silence. There is much to see.

There is the fire which smoulders on the great hearth until roused by the bellows. Then it bursts into flame, scattering a shower of sparks and lighting up the quiet faces of the men who sit round the walls. There is the mighty anvil on which the great hammers ring with a musical clang as the hot iron is beaten into the required shape. There is the water-tank into which the dulling metal is dropped with a splash and a sizzle. There are the pieces of iron of all shapes and sizes from which the expert eye of the blacksmith can select, in a few minutes, the one best suited to his purpose.

While the smith is working, we sit and listen to the roar of the bellows, the ring of the anvil, the hissing of the tank, the softly-spoken word which soothes a startled young colt whose hooves are being shaped for the first time for the heavy iron shoes.

Horse-shoes, gate-hinges, parts of ploughs and tractors—our blacksmith handles them all with ease and skill. His father and grandfather before him worked in the forge. His son will carry on the work in the time to come.

Questions

1. What is the blacksmith's name ?
2. Where does he work ?
3. What do the neighbours like to do on winter evenings ?
4. What is to be seen in the forge ?
5. What sounds are to be heard in the forge ?
6. What use does the blacksmith make of (a) the bellows, (b) the anvil, (c) the water-tank ?
7. Explain these words : neighbours, hearth, soothe.

8. What part of speech is each word in the following sentences? Tell all you know about the nouns, pronouns, adjectives and adverbs in the sentences: (a) Our blacksmith does his work skilfully. (b) A neighbour once brought a young horse to the forge. (c) The fire lighted up the quiet faces of the men who sat there. (d) Sometimes they talk ; sometimes they sit in silence and watch the smith's work.
9. Analyse sentences (a) and (b) of Question 8.

B. Write an account of a visit to a factory, workshop, creamery, or farm.

C. THERE

Note that the adverb *there* is sometimes used to introduce a sentence : *There* is no one here. *There* is much to see.
HOW AND WHAT

Note that the adverbs *how* and *what* are sometimes used to exclaim or express surprise : *How* kind of you! *What* a foolish boy you are !

D. THE COMPARISON OF ADVERBS

Adverbs ending in *ly* form their Comparative and Superlative by adding *more* and *most* : *wisely, more wisely, most wisely*. Note, however, that the adverb *early* has *earlier* for its Comparative.

E. The same word occurs in each of the following pairs of sentences : say what the word is and what part of speech it is in each sentence :

1. (a) The early bird catches the worm. (b) Come early.
2. (a) It's a long way to Tipperary. (b) Have you been waiting long ?
3. (a) I saw her passing by. (b) We passed by your window.
4. (a) He sat on the chair. (b) We were just looking on.
5. (a) Come in. (b) It is in the box.

6. (a) Look up. (b) The mouse ran up the clock.
7. (a) He was here before I came. (b) Have you seen that before?
8. (a) May the best man win! (b) He works best at night.

F. Write an adverb instead of the words in italics in each of the following sentences:

1. They sat *without speaking*.
2. The blacksmith did his work *with great care*.
3. The soldiers stepped out *at a smart pace*.
4. They listened *with great joy*.
5. The mother spoke to the child *with affection*.
6. That happened *on two occasions*.

G. Add suitable adverbs to the following sentences:

1. They waited —. 2. He ate —. 3. They sang —.
4. He yawned —. 5. Rain fell —. 6. She laughed —.

H. Supply suitable Adverbs of Degree in the following sentences: (Do not use the word *very* in more than one of the sentences.)

1. This tea is — weak. 2. You are — right. 3. That is — wrong. 4. It is — cold. 5. The child is — ill. 6. I was — doubtful. 7. He is a — clever man. 8. That is a — beautiful picture. 9. That is — bad. 10. You are looking — well. 11. His face was — black. 12. — many cooks spoil the broth.

I. " THERE " AND " THEIR "

Remember that *there* is an adverb and that *their* is an adjective.

Fill in each blank in these sentences with the word " there " or " their ":

1. — are four children in — family. 2. The dogs lay — with — heads in — paws. 3. — is nothing —. 4. They keep — books — in the cupboard. 5. The swallows make — nests —. 6. — is no one in — room.

CRANN

Tá crann sa páirc:
Crann beag deas.

Tá nead sa crann:
Nead beag deas.

Tá ub sa nead:
Ub beag deas.

Tá éan san ub:
Éan beag deas.

An t-éan san ub,
An t-ub sa nead,
An nead sa crann,
An crann sa páirc,
Agus bláta buí
ag fás mór-timpeall.

JESUS ASCENDS INTO HEAVEN

*182. What will Christ say to the just on the last day ?

Christ will say to the just on the last day : *Come, ye blessed of my Father, possess you the kingdom prepared for you from the foundation of the world* (*Matt.* xxv, 34).

183. How will the bodies of the damned rise ?

The bodies of the damned will not rise glorious, but they will be immortal, to share in the everlasting punishment of the soul.

*184. What will Christ say to the wicked on the last day ?

Christ will say to the wicked on the last day : *Depart from me, you cursed, into everlasting fire, which was prepared for the devil and his angels* (*Matt.* xxv, 41).

*185. What does life everlasting mean ?

Life everlasting means that, if we serve God faithfully in this life, we shall see, love and enjoy Him for ever in heaven.

*186. What is the meaning of the word Amen ?

By the word *Amen* is meant *so be it* : at the end of the Apostles' Creed it expresses our firm belief in all the doctrines that the Creed contains.

CHAPTER 13

COUNTIES AND TOWNS

COUNTIES OF ULSTER (ULAIDH)

Donegal (Dún na nGall)

Lifford (Leifear): Shirt- and collar-making.

Ballyshannon (Béal Átha Seannaidh): on the Erne. Salmon fisheries. Electricity-generating station.

Letterkenny (Leitir Ceanainn): Hosiery, sweet-making. Bacon factory.

Donegal (Dún na nGall): Shirt- and collar-making, woollens.

Derry (Doire)

Derry (Doire): on the Foyle. Shipbuilding, shirt- and collar-making, motor-tyre fabric.

Coleraine (Cúil Rathain): Distilling, shirt-making.

Limavady (Léim an Mhadaidh): Flax markets.

Antrim (Aontroim)

Belfast (Béal Feirste): on the Lagan. Population 399,000. Shipbuilding, linen, tobacco, rope-making, etc. Seat of Six-County Government.

Carrickfergus (Carraig Fhearghasa): Salt, rayon.

Lisburn (Lios na gCearrbhach): Linen.

Ballymena (Baile Meánach): Linen, tobacco.

Larne (Latharna): Paper mills, Packet station for Stranraer.

Down (An Dún)

Downpatrick (Dún Pádraig) : Burial place of St. Patrick.

Newry (Iúr Cinn Trá) : Export trade in agricultural produce. Flour mills. Cotton weaving.

Newtownards (Baile Ard Uladh) : Linen, cotton.

Banbridge (Droichead na Banna) : on the upper Bann. Lace curtains, footwear.

Bangor (Beannchar) : Linen. Holiday resort.

Armagh (Ard Mhacha)

Armagh (Ard Mhacha) : Ecclesiastical capital of Ireland.

Lurgan (An Lurgain) : Linen.

Portadown (Port an Dúnáin) : Linen, cider. Centre of fruit-growing district.

Monaghan (Muineachán)

Monaghan (Muineachán) : Bacon, boots, leather.

Clones (Cluain Eois) : Clothing, rail-junction.

Carrickmacross (Carraig Mhachaire Rois) : Fruit-canning.

Cavan (An Cabhán)

Cavan (An Cabhán) : Rail junction.

Cootehill (Muinchille) : Woollens.

Belturbet (Béal Tairbirt) : Market town.

Fermanagh (Fir Mhanach)

Enniskillen (Inis Ceithleann) : Noted for scenery.

Lisnaskea (Lios na Scéithe) : Market town.

Tyrone (Tír Eoghain)

Omagh (An Ómaigh) : Flax markets.

Dungannon (Dún Geanainn) : Woollens, bricks.

Strabane (An Srath Bán) : Clothing.

Cookstown (An Chorr Chríochach) : Hosiery, woollens.

COUNTIES OF MUNSTER (AN MHUMHAIN)

Waterford (Port Láirge)

Waterford (Port Láirge): Important port. Brewing, butter, margarine, bacon, glass, paper, and ropes.

Dungarvan (Dún Garbhán): Tanning, fisheries, chocolate crumb.

Lismore (Lios Mór): on the Blackwater.

Cork (Corcaigh)

Cork (Corcaigh): Third city in Ireland. Export trade. Noted for butter, margarine, hosiery, motorcars and tractors, shipbuilding, and oil-refining.

Cobh (Cóbh): Port of call for Atlantic liners.

Bandon (Droichead na Bandan): Market town.

Fermoy (Mainistir Fhear Maighe): Woollens.

Mallow (Malla): Sugar factory.

Youghal (Eochaill): Cotton-spinning, textiles, carpets, fishing, holiday resort.

Kinsale (Cionn tSáile): Fishing.

Kerry (Ciarraí)

Tralee (Trá Lí): Hosiery, bacon-curing, boots.

Killarney (Cill Áirne): Tourist centre. Manufactures boots and heavy cranes.

Dingle (An Daingean): Fishing.

Listowel (Lios Tuathail): Market town.

Clare (An Clár)

Ennis (Inis): Laces.

Kilrush (Cill Rois): Slate and marble.

Killaloe (Cill Dalua): Cardboard boxes. Slate quarries. Eel fisheries.

Kilkee (Cill Chaoidhe): Seaside resort.

Limerick (Luimneach)

Limerick (Luimneach): Bacon, flour, lace, biscuits, cement, wagon-building (C.I.E.), tanning.

Rathkeale (Ráth Caola): Market town.

Newcastle West (An Caisleán Nua): Market town.

Tipperary (Tiobraid Árann)

Clonmel (Cluain Meala): Bacon, meat-canning, cider, brewing, woollens, boots and shoes.

Tipperary (Tiobraid Árann): Linoleum, gloves.

Nenagh (Aonach): Aluminium ware and bakelite.

Thurles (Durlas): on the Suir. Sugar factory; barley markets; rail junction.

Cashel (Caiseal): Once the seat of the Kings of Munster. Ruins of historic cathedral.

Carrick-on-Suir (Carraig na Siúire): Brewing, tanning.

Roscrea (Ros Cré): Bacon-curing; trout farm.

COUNTIES OF LEINSTER (LAIGHIN)

Louth (Lú)

Dundalk (Dún Dealgan): Brewing, tobacco, motor-cars, boots and shoes.

Drogheda (Droichead Átha): Woollens, cotton-spinning, cement, boots, margarine.

Ardee (Áth Fhirdhia): Agricultural implements, furniture, cotton-weaving.

Carlingford (Cairlinn): Oyster fisheries.

Meath (An Mhidhe)

Navan (An Uaimh): Woollens, carpets, furniture.

Kells (Ceannanas Mór): Boot factory and tannery.

Trim (Áth Troim): Fancy leather.

Dublin (Baile Átha Cliath)

Dublin (Baile Átha Cliath): Brewing, distilling, biscuit-making, and many other industries. (Pop., 570,000.) The capital of Ireland, and its principal distributing centre.

Dún Laoghaire: Mail packet station for Holyhead. Tobacco and cigarettes. Slippers.

Balbriggan (Baile Brigín): Hosiery, linen, cotton.

Wicklow (Cill Mhantáin)

Wicklow (Cill Mhantáin): Artificial manures, fishing.
Arklow (Inbhear Mór): Fishing, pottery.
Bray (Bré): Tourist resort. Electric bulbs and glassware.

Wexford (Loch Garman)

Wexford (Loch Garman): Flour mills, hosiery, agricultural implements.
New Ross (Ros Mhic Thriúin): Milling, brewing.
Enniscorthy (Inis Córthaigh): Agricultural machinery, bacon, cutlery, brewing.

Kildare (Cill Dara)

Naas (Nás): Cotton, rayon. Protective clothing.
Athy (Áth Í): Motor bodies, asbestos, wallboard.
Maynooth (Má Nuad): Ecclesiastical college.
Kildare (Cill Dara): Wallpaper.
Newbridge (Droichead Nua): Cutlery, ropes, carpets.

Carlow (Ceatharlach)

Carlow (Ceatharlach): Sugar, boots, razor-blades.
Muine Bheag: On the Barrow.

Kilkenny (Cill Chainnigh)

Kilkenny (Cill Chainnigh): Brewing, woollens, marble.
Callan (Callainn): Market town.
Castlecomer (Caisleán an Chomair): Coal.

Laois

Portlaoise: Woollens and worsteds.
Portarlington (Cúil an tSúdaire): Sports goods.
Mountmellick (Móinteach Mílic): Lace.

Offaly (Uíbh Fhailí)

Tullamore (An Tulach Mhór): Distilling, bacon-curing, woollen and worsted yarn.
Birr (Biorra): Boots.

Edenderry (Éadan Doire): Furniture.

Westmeath (An Iar-Mhidhe)

Mullingar (An Muileann Cearr): Tobacco, woollens, livestock mart, creamery.

Athlone (Áth Luain): Woollens, cotton, linen.

Longford (Longfort)

Longford (Longfort): Furniture, rayon cloth.

Granard (Gránard): Market town.

Edgeworthstown (Meathas Troim): Market town.

COUNTIES OF CONNACHT (CONNACHTA)

Galway (Gaillimh)

Galway (Gaillimh): Fisheries, woollens, marble, millinery, agricultural implements. University college.

Tuam (Tuaim): Sugar factory.

Ballinasloe (Béal Átha na Sluaighe): Cattle-, horse-, and sheep fairs. Boots and shoes.

Mayo (Maigh Eo)

Castlebar (Caisleán an Bharraigh): Bacon factory, meat-canning, hats and millinery.

Ballina (Béal an Átha): Milling.

Westport (Cathair na Mart): Fishing, thread.

Sligo (Sligeach)

Sligo (Sligeach): Bacon-curing, iron foundry, textiles.

Ballymote (Baile an Mhóta): Market town.

Collooney (Cail Mhuine): Rail junction. Woollens.

Tubbercurry (Tobar an Choire): Joinery.

Leitrim (Liatroim)

Carrick-on-Shannon (Cora Droma Rúisc): Market town.

Roscommon (Ros Comáin)

Roscommon (Ros Comáin): Market town.

Boyle (Mainistir na Búille): Market town.

Ballaghaderreen (Bealach an Doirín): Bacon.

A STORY OF SAINT BRIGID

The King of Leinster had a pet fox, of which he was very fond. It was as playful as a kitten, and it had as many tricks as a circus dog.

One day, the fox escaped, and ran into the woods, where it was killed by a poor woodman.

When the King heard that his fox was dead, his anger knew no bounds. The woodman begged for mercy, but the King would not listen to him.

"Take him away," he said to his soldiers. "To-morrow at sunrise he shall die."

Some of the woodman's friends went to Saint Brigid then, and asked her to save his life. The good saint set out at once for the palace. On her way to the palace she saw a wild fox in the woods.

"Come with me, little fox," she said.

Then the wild fox jumped into the saint's chariot and nestled at her feet; and it sat quietly in the chariot when Brigid went into the palace to plead with the King.

At first, the King would not listen to Saint Brigid.

"This man must die," he cried. "He has killed the best fox in all Ireland."

Saint Brigid smiled, and shook her head.

"The best fox in all Ireland is at the palace door. Take it in place of the fox you have lost."

Brigid called to the wild fox, and it came at her bidding. It had never been trained, but when she spoke to it it did more tricks, and

better tricks, than the King's fox had ever done.

When the King saw this he agreed to set the woodman free, and to take the wild fox in place of the one he had lost.

II

Some days later, the wild fox escaped from the palace. It ran through the woods and the fields, with the King and his horsemen close behind; and it did not stop until it reached Saint Brigid's convent and nestled again at her feet.

Brigid came to the convent gates to meet the King.

"A gift is a gift," said the King. "You gave me a fox, and now you have taken it back."

"You know the rule," said

Brigid. "When any hunted thing enters our walls it is safe from those who follow it. Life belongs to God, not to men. You were wrong to seek the life of the poor woodman."

"I was wrong," said the King humbly. "Keep your fox, good Saint Brigid."

"It is not mine to keep," said Brigid. "Let it go back to the woods and lead the life that God meant it to lead."

At this the little fox rose to its feet, ran swiftly out of the convent, and was soon lost to sight

The King and his horsemen rode back to the palace, and Brigid knelt to praise the good God who watches over all things, great and small.

Dóchas Linn Naomh Pádraig

Dóchas linn Naomh Pádraig
Aspal mór na hÉireann,
Ainm oirirc gléigeal,
Solas mór an tsaoil é.
Sé a chloígh na draoithe,
Croíthe dúra, gan aon mhaith,
D'ísligh dream an díomais
Trí neart Dé ar dtréanfhlaith.

Sléibhte, gleannta, mánna,
'S bailte móra na hÉireann,
Ghlan sé iad go deo dúinn
Míle glóir dár Naomh dhil.
Iarraimid ort, a Phádraig,
Guí orainne, Gaela
Dia linn lá is oíche,
'S Pádraig, Aspal Éireann.

Ní fios cé a chum

XII—Little Rules for Health and Happiness

1. If I want to be happy
      And quick on my toes,
   I must bite my food slowly
      And breathe through my nose.

2. I must press back my shoulders
      And hold up my head,
   And *not* close my window
      When going to bed.

3. I must soap my bath-flannel,
      And scrub myself—so !—
   I must then take a towel
      And rub till I glow.

4. I must never be idle
   And loll in my chair,
   Nor shout like a demon
   And act like a bear.

5. I must play and not fidget,
   Read books and not flop ;
   Begin all with a purpose,
   And know when to stop.

6. I must love what is noble
   And do what is kind ;
   I must strengthen my body
   And tidy my mind.

7. And so, to be healthy
   And free from all cares,
   I must do all I've told you,
   And *mean* all my prayers.

THE SHADOW PEOPLE

OLD lame Bridget doesn't hear
  Fairy music in the grass,
When the gloaming's on the mere
And the shadow people pass:
Never hears their slow grey feet
Coming from the village street,
Just beyond the parson's wall,
Where the clover globes are sweet
And the mushroom's parasol
Opens in the moonlit rain.
Every night I hear them call
From their long and merry train.
Old lame Bridget says to me,
"It is just your fancy, child."
She cannot believe I see
Laughing faces in the wild,
Hands that twinkle in the sedge
Bowing at the water's edge
Where the finny minnows quiver,
Shaping on a blue wave's ledge
Bubble foam to sail the river.
And the sunny hands to me
Beckon ever, beckon ever:
Oh! I would be wild and free
And with the shadow people be.

FRANCIS LEDWIDGE.
Complete Poems.

DUBLIN AIRPORT

LONG before the advance of science made it possible for him to fly, man must have envied the birds their freedom of the air. Legend tells of his various attempts to imitate the birds—attempts, however, which came to nothing. It was not till the eighteenth century, with the invention of the balloon, that human flight became a practicable thing.

But the balloon, even when it could be steered, proved slow and clumsy, and was too much at the mercy of contrary winds and bad weather.

To the brothers, Orville and Wilbur Wright, bicycle makers in Ohio, America, the world is indebted for the construction of the first aeroplane. In 1900 Wilbur Wright glided for short distances through the air in a machine closely resembling a box-kite.

A few years later, in 1903, the Wrights attached a motor engine to their machine; and in December of that year they succeeded in making four short flights. In 1905 they travelled twenty-four miles in one flight, and by 1908 they had made a machine which was able to remain in the air for over an hour.

In July, 1909, a Frenchman, Bleriot, flew across the English Channel. A year later another Frenchman, Paulhan, flew from London to Manchester. These feats, remarkable as they were when flying was in its infancy, were soon eclipsed by far longer flights: from Newfoundland to Ireland, from England to Australia and to Cape Town, from Ireland to Labrador, and from Ireland to Newfoundland. In each of these last two flights an Irishman took part. It was not long till civil aviation on a large scale began and the great cities of the world were linked by air.

No progressive country can afford to ignore this very modern mode of travel. Most countries now recognise the importance of the aeroplane, and do all they can to encourage flying. In our own country Shannon Airport and Dublin Airport are among the finest in the world.

The Company of Aer Lingus was formed on May 22, 1936, and five days later its first flight, from Dublin to Bristol, took place. In those early days of Irish civil aviation the home base was at Baldonnel, the Irish Army Air Corps field, south-west of Dublin. In 1937 construction work was begun on a site at Collinstown, seven miles north of Dublin. The main structures were completed in 1940, and that year saw the first flight from the new Dublin Airport.

The main Terminal Building curves in a graceful arc four hundred feet long, and was designed by a young Irish architect. It is built of reinforced concrete faced with white cement, and stands on the eastern edge of the airfield. The ground approach to it is by double carriage ways and footpaths, bordered by neat grass plots studded with bright flower beds. One of the most remarkable features of the Terminal

Building is its wide expanse of window on the airfield side.

The main hall, two storeys high in front, and faced with marble, contains a spacious lounge, restaurants, traffic and inquiry rooms, and various offices. The building is centrally heated throughout, and the arrival and departure of planes are announced by loud speaker.

Perched high on the top of the Terminal Building are the control tower and radio room, glassed in on all sides and commanding an unobstructed view of the great concrete runways and the surrounding countryside. Adjoining the main building are the huge hangars and workshops.

Dublin Airport stands 215 feet above sea level, and therefore normally above the reach of fog. This permits service to continue uninterrupted even when unfavourable weather conditions cause operations at many other airports to be suspended.

Many a traveller now steps into an aeroplane as casually as he would step on to a train or on board a ship. Air travel has become comparatively safe, and its speed, its cleanliness, and its convenience and comfort commend it to those who have tried it.

By air one can get from Dublin to Shannon or to Liverpool in an hour, to Glasgow in an hour and twenty-minutes, to London in two hours, and to Paris in four hours, fifteen minutes. Even a few years ago, who would have thought it possible?

WHICH WAS THE STRONGER?

One day the north wind was passing over the land.

"What can be so strong as I am?" it cried. "I am stronger even than the sun."

"Oh, no, I think not," said the sun.

"Well, let us try which of us is the stronger," was the reply.

Just then a man was walking up a hill beside a loaded wagon. He was wearing a long thick cloak, or mantle.

"Let us see which of us can force this man to strip off his cloak," cried the north wind.

"Very well," said the sun, "be it so."

Then the wind blew a fierce blast. It filled the sky with dust. The man was nearly lifted off his feet. His mantle went flying and flapping, and was almost torn off his back. He stopped for a moment.

"He is going to fling off his cloak," cried the north wind. But the man only fastened the mantle more tightly round his body, and then walked on with his horse and wagon.

Now it was the sun's turn for the trial of his strength. He shone forth in all his glory.

"What a splendid evening it is, after that gust of wind!" said the man; "it is now quite bright and warm."

But by and by it grew so hot that he had to open his mantle. Then the evening became hotter still, and the man was panting as he walked. "I cannot stand this," he cried, and at last he pulled off his thick mantle and put it on the wagon.

One sees, therefore, that the quiet power of the sun was stronger than all the rage and fury of the north wind.

Æsop.

I like to see a thing I know
  Has not been seen before;
That's why I cut my apple through
  To look into the core.

It's nice to think, though many an
    eye
  Has seen the ruddy skin,
Mine is the very first to spy
  The five brown pips within.

EXERCISE 40

Revision

*(1) (a) Find the sum of £9 14s. 10½d. ; £17 12s. 9d. ; £1 15s. 4½d. ; £129 16s. 8d. ; £7 13s. 9¼d. ; £37 15s. 8½d.

(b) Multiply the sum by 11.

(2) Find the cost of fencing the four sides of a rectangular garden 154 ft. by 95 ft. at 5s. 6d. per yard.

(3) Find the value of 24½% of £48 16s. to the nearest shilling. (Work decimally.)

(4) Press report : "Almost 100,000 tons of special cement were imported into this country during the first 4 months of 1950 at a cost of £545,000." Find the cost in £ s. per ton. (Work decimally.)

(5) How many lb. of seed will be required to sow 5 ac. 1 rd. 30 sq. per. at the rate of 224 lb. to the acre ?

(6) Simplify $\dfrac{53 \cdot 5249}{3 \cdot 8 \times \cdot 55}$ correct to one place of decimals.

(7) A programme for a motor-cycle race gave the following : 25,560 ÷ lap time in seconds = lap speed in m.p.h. Find the average speed of a rider whose lap time was 5 min. 51 sec. (Give answer correct to two decimal places.)

(8) If electricity costs 5·6d. per unit for lighting and 12s. 6d. per 1,000 units for heat, find the total cost of 240 units for lighting and 2,500 units for heat.

(9) A man leaves home at 9.20 a.m. to drive 15 miles to the city. If he drives at an average speed of 25 m.p.h., at what time does he reach the city ?

(10) The area of a field is 4·9 Statute acres. Change this into Irish acres to the nearest sq. per.
(1 Statute acre = 0·617 Irish acres.)

(11) x stands for a certain number. **67·5** times x is equal to the difference between **56·5** and **0·475**. Find the value of x.

(12) A man bought a house for £1,750. He let it for £120 per year but had to pay out £41 5s. for the year in ground rent, rates, etc. What was his percentage profit on his outlay ?

(13) How many cwt. of potatoes at 1s. 7d. per stone can be bought for £12 15s. ? (Answer correct to the nearest cwt.)

*(14) Find the cost of producing **525** gallons of milk at **5·12**d. per gallon.

*(15) Add **16** cwt. **7** st. **7** lb. ; **14** cwt. **5** st. **2** lb. ; **6** cwt. **3** st. **11** lb. ; **14** cwt. **7** st. **10** lb. ; **27** cwt. **1** st. **7** lb. ; **18** cwt. **5** st. **4** lb. ; **16** cwt. **7** st. **1** lb.

(16) Find the rent of a field of **4** ac. **3** rds. **20** sq. per. at £5 **10**s. **6**d. per acre.

(17) Find the Simple Interest on £100 for **5** months at **6**% and from that find the interest on £760 for the same time and at the same rate.

*(18) Multiply £4 **18**s. **6**d. by $11\frac{11}{12}$.

(19) Make out a bill for the following :
$4\frac{1}{2}$ lb. butter at 2s. 8d. per lb. ; $\frac{3}{4}$ stone of sugar at 7d. per lb. ; **42** bottles of milk at $5\frac{1}{2}$d. each ; **45** eggs at 4s. 6d. per doz.; $1\frac{1}{2}$ lb. back rashers at 3s. 5d. per lb. ; $\frac{1}{4}$ lb. tobacco at 1s. $10\frac{1}{2}$d. per oz.

(20) Cement is bought at £4 **3**s. **6**d. per ton, plus **7**s. **6**d. carriage, and sold at **6**s. **3**d. per bag (**1** cwt.). (a) Find the profit on the sale of **10** tons. (b) Find the percentage profit to one decimal place.

(21) Find the value of **0·499** × **33·8** ÷ **7·9** correct to two decimal places. Give a rough estimate first (·5 × 34 ÷ 8).

(22) Find the Simple Interest for **9** months at **4**% per annum on **£1,025** and then find the interest on £102 **10**s. for the same time and at the same rate.

(23) What sum of money will produce **£57 15**s. at Simple Interest for **3** years at $3\frac{1}{2}$% per annum ?

(24) When the rate of exchange is **£1 = 2·8** dollars, find to the nearest penny the value of **1,350** dollars.

(25) Find the value of a load of sheet lead weighing **3** tons **5** cwt. **3** qrs. at £7 **15**s. per ton.

(26) What will **£257 10**s. amount to at Simple Interest for **2** years **4** months at $2\frac{1}{2}$% per annum ?

(27) Find in £ s. d., correct to the nearest penny, the value of **£16 18**s. × **8·57**. (Make a rough estimate first, say **£17** × $8\frac{1}{2}$.)

*(28) Take $\frac{2}{3}$ from the sum of the two fractions nearest to $\frac{7}{8}$ that have **72** as denominator.

(29) A ship arrived in port with **876** tons of coal. Find the value of the cargo at £4 **18**s. **9**d. per ton (Practice).

(30) An advertisement read : " Carpenters wanted. **3**s. $2\frac{1}{2}$d. per hour + **6**d. per day tool money + **38**s. **6**d. per week country money." If a carpenter, on these terms, worked on **6** days of the week for a total of **44** hours, what would he earn in **13** weeks.

(31) Suits in a Dublin shop were marked in dollars for American visitors. One suit was marked " **13** guineas or **$38·22**." What was the rate of exchange ?

(32) Estimate the yield of turnips from a field of **4** ac. **3** rds. **16** sq. per. at the rate of **15** tons per acre.

*(33) (a) Express **12**s. $8\frac{3}{4}$d. as a decimal of **£1** correct to four decimal places.

    (b) Using this result, find the approximate cost of **100** articles at **12**s. $8\frac{3}{4}$d. each.

Part I

THE CREED

CHAPTER I

GOD: HIS NATURE AND PERFECTIONS

* 1. Who made the world ?
    God made the world.

* 2. Who is God ?
    God is our Father in heaven, the Creator and Lord of all things.

* 3. Why do we call God our Father ?
    We call God our Father, because He gave us life and provides for us with fatherly care.

* 4. Had God a beginning ?
    God had no beginning : He always was, and always will be ; He is eternal.

* 5. Can God do all things ?
    God can do all things ; He is almighty.

* 6. Where is God ?
    God is everywhere, but in a special way He is in heaven, where He is seen by the angels and saints.

Note: The * indicates the easier questions which should be memorised by the smaller children.

* 7. If God is everywhere, why do we not see Him ?

We do not see God, because He is a spirit, and therefore cannot be seen with bodily eyes.

* 8. Does God see us ?

God sees us, for nothing is hidden from his all-seeing eye (*Heb.* iv, 13).

* 9. Does God know all things ?

God knows all things, past, present and to come, even our most secret thoughts and actions.

*10. Is God holy, just and merciful ?

Yes, God is infinitely holy, just and merciful.

*11. Why do we call God just ?

We call God just, because He will reward the good and punish the wicked.

ÆSOP'S FABLES.

PART IV.

THE OLD MAN AND HIS ASS.

1. An old man and his son were driving an ass to the market to sell.

"What a fool is this fellow," says a man upon the road, "to be trudging it on foot with his son, that his ass may go light!"

The old man hearing this, set his boy upon the ass, and went whistling by his side.

2. "Why, you young rogue!" cries a second

man to the boy, " is it fit for you to be riding, while your poor aged father is on foot ? "

The father, upon this rebuke, took down his boy from the ass and mounted himself.

3. " Do you see," says a third, " how the lazy old knave rides along upon his beast, whilst his poor little boy is almost crippled with walking ? "

The old man no sooner heard this, than he took up his son behind him.

4. " Pray, honest friend," says a fourth, " is that ass your own ? "

" Yes," says the man.

"One would not have thought so," replied the other, " by your loading him as you do without mercy. You and your son are better able to carry the poor beast than he is to carry you."

5. " Anything you please," says the owner. Then he and his son dismounting, tied the legs of the ass together, and by the help of a pole tried to carry him upon their shoulders over the bridge that led to the town.

6. This was so amusing a sight that the people came in crowds to laugh at it ; till the ass, not liking the too great courtesy of his master, burst asunder the cords which tied him, slipped from the pole, and tumbled into the river.

7. The poor old man made the best of his way home, ashamed and vexed, that, by trying to please everybody, he had pleased nobody, and lost his ass into the bargain.

A RIDDLE

(**W**)hat runs, but has no feet to walk?

(**A**)nd tells us much, but cannot talk?

(**T**)hat has two hands, a face quite round,

(**C**)an make a little tick-tock sound?

(**H**)ere in these lines its name is found.

HOW SHOULD WE PRAY?

When I kneel down my prayers to
    say,
I must not think of toys or play.
No! I must think what I should be
To please God who is kind to me;
To please my parents, and to do
What's good and right and say
    what's true.
For always God delights to see
Good little children such as we,
Whose hearts (like angels' hearts
    above)
Are full of peace and full of love.

Lady Flora Hastings.

I.W. BEG. BK.

THE NIGHT SKY

All day long
    The sun shines bright;
The moon and the stars
    Come out at night.

The moon and the stars,
    So far, far away,
Send us their light,
    Till the break of day.

When the darkness falls,
    They line the skies,
And look down on the world
    With old, old, eyes.

THE ROBIN AND THE PUSSY-CAT.

Little Robin Redbreast
  Sat upon a tree ;
Up went Pussy-cat,
  And down went he ;

Down came Pussy-cat,
  And away Robin ran ;
Says Little Robin Red-
    breast,
  "Catch me if you can."

Little Robin Redbreast
  Perched upon a wall ;
Pussy-cat jumped after
    him
    And nearly
    got a fall.

Little Robin chirped and sang,
  And what did Pussy say ?
Pussy-cat said, " Mew, mew,"
  And Robin flew away.

We had tea

Tom said, "We had tea.
  We had bread and jam."

Mary said, "We had apples."

Billy said, "Spot had bread
  and milk."

Tom said, "Spot ran
    after the pig.
  Spot ran after the hen."

Mary said, "The dog ran
    after Spot.
  Spot ran and ran and ran."

We had a ride

Tom said, "We had a ride
on the pony."

Mary said, "We had a ride
on the hay cart."

Tom said, "We went
to toss the hay."

Billy said, "Spot can
toss the hay.

Up, up, up, high."

THE ROBIN'S SONG

GOD bless every field and furrow,
Every stream and rabbit burrow,
Hill and stone, and flower and tree,
Everything that I can see.

Bless the sun and bless the sleet,
Bless each lane, and every street,
Bless the minnow and the whale,
Bless the rainbow and the hail,
Bless the wing and bless the fin,
Bless the air I travel in.

Bless the nest and bless the leaf,
Bless the good man and the thief,
Bless the mill and bless the mouse,
Bless the miller's little house,

Bless the earth and bless the sea —
God bless you and God bless me.

" Bless the wing and bless the fin "
means " bless the birds and the . . . ."

HOT CROSS BUNS

Hot cross buns!
Hot cross buns!
One a penny,
Two a penny,
Hot cross buns!
If your daughters do not like them,
Give them to your sons;
One a penny,
Two a penny,
Hot cross buns!

úlla agus milseáin

Fuair Seán réal.
Fuair Síle réal.

" Ceannóió mé úlla," arsa Seán.
" Ceannóió mé milseáin," arsa Síle.
Rit Seán agus Síle
    go dtí an siopa.

Ceannaig Seán úlla.
Ceannaig Síle milseáin.

Táinig Seán agus Síle abaile.

Ṫuʒ Seán úll ꝺo Ṁamaí.
Ṫuʒ sé úll ꝺo Ḋeaꝺí.
Ṫuʒ sé úll ꝺo Ṡíle.

" Ʒura maiṫ aʒaꞇ," arsa Ṁamaí.
" Ʒura maiṫ aʒaꞇ," arsa Ḋeaꝺí.
" Ʒura maiṫ aʒaꞇ," arsa Síle.

Ṫuʒ Síle milseán ꝺo Ṁamaí.
Ṫuʒ sí milseán ꝺo Ḋeaꝺí.
Ṫuʒ sí milseán ꝺo Ṡeán.

" Ʒura maiṫ aʒaꞇ," arsa Ṁamaí.
" Ʒura maiṫ aʒaꞇ," arsa Ḋeaꝺí.
" Ʒura maiṫ aʒaꞇ," arsa Seán.

YOU CAN'T PLEASE EVERYONE

Two ducks came waddling down the lane;
Said one to the other, "What beautiful
    rain!
I hope that the sun never shines again!"

Two little people with heads of brown,
Looked out at the rain with a scowl and
    a frown;
Said one to the other, "It's still coming
    down!"

The Clerk of the Weather scratched his
    head:
"You can't please everyone," he said.

BUTTERCUP GOLD.

There are rich little boys in the big
    wide world,
  And rich little girls, I'm told ;
But the poorest child is the richest
    child
  If he gathers buttercup gold.

God puts it out in the grassy fields
  For anyone passing there.
Come, gather the buttercup gold with
    me,
  There's more than enough to spare.

IN TOWN

Mother and Tom and Mary are in
town.

They came in the train.

The train went very fast.

" Faster than the wind," said Tom.

They had tea in a tea-shop.

They had cake for tea, and then
Tom and Mary had ice-cream.

Tom and Mary like ice-cream.

Then they went to a shop. They got a new hat for Mary and new shoes for Tom.

"I like my new hat," said Mary.

"I like my new shoes," said Tom.

"Now we must get toys for Pat and Billy," said Mother.

They got a bat and a ball for Pat and a toy train for Billy.

And what about Baby?

Baby got a little drum.

Baby bangs the drum all day long.

Rub-a-dub-a-dub!

Baby likes to bang his drum.

THE SEASONS.

Sing a song of seasons,
　　Something good in all:
Flowers in the Springtime,
　　Apples in the Fall,

Bright long days in Summer,
　　Rest for man and beast,
Fun at home in Winter,
　　And our Christmas feast.

THE TINKER MAN

Dan, Dan, the tinker man,
He goes the road in a caravan.

Dan, Dan, the tinker man,
He hammers away on an old
tin can.

Dan, Dan, the tinker man,
He has a mare called Mary Ann.

Dan, Dan, the tinker man,
He whipped the mare and away
she ran.

THE BALLOON MAN.

One day a strange man came down the lane that led to the farm where Cormac lived. This man had come from Galway and had toy balloons to sell to the children as he passed along the roads.

In one hand he had a toy trumpet; in the other he held a big bunch of balloons. Each balloon was on a tiny cord of its own, and all the little cords were tied fast to a thick cord which the man held in his hand. Some of the balloons were pink; some were blue; others were yellow. Oh, they did look bright and gay as they floated in the air !

Cormac ran out to look at them. Just as he reached the gate, the balloon man put the trumpet to his lips and gave a long, long blow. Out ran Billy from his shed. The sound of the trumpet had wakened him from a quiet doze and he was not pleased at all. Down went his head, ready to butt. Oh ! what a bad, bad look Billy Goat had in his eye as he made a dash for the balloon man.

" Don't go," said Cormac, to the man ; " he will not hurt you. He only does it for fun."

But the balloon man did not wait to see. Those horns of Billy's were long and sharp and were much too near him. He just gave one shout of wild alarm and made off as fast as his legs would go. Billy Goat went racing after him. In his haste to get away, the poor man let go the cord that held the bunch of balloons. Cormac picked it up for fear the balloons might blow away.

It was tea-time before Billy Goat came home. No one knows whether he caught up with the balloon man or not, for the balloon man never came back to tell. Cormac, like an honest boy, kept the balloons for their rightful owner as safe as he could. But they did not last long. Toy balloons, you know, are flimsy things, and they all burst, one by one.

SUAS

Tá Seán agus Síle
   ag dul suas an cnoc,
Suas an cnoc, suas an cnoc.
Tá Seán agus Síle
   ag dul suas an cnoc,
Suas an cnoc go mall.

C.E.

a b c d e f g h i j k l m

a b c d e f g h i j k l m

n o p q r s t u v w x y z

n o p q r s t u v w x y z

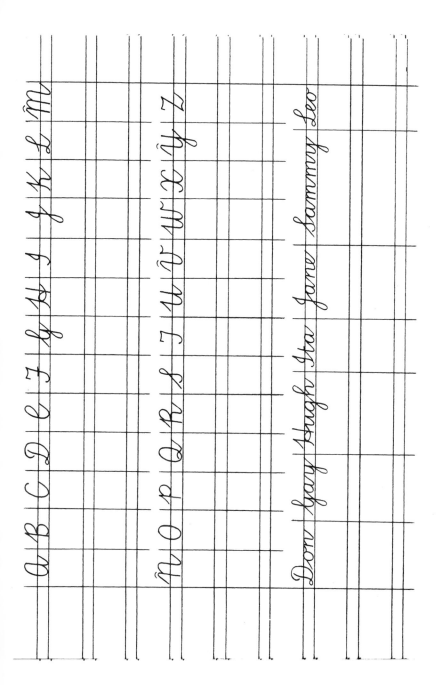

COURTESY AND POLITENESS.

superse'des, does away with, takes the place of.

perpet'uated, continued without ceasing.

affecta'tion, an attempt to assume what is not natural or real.

supercil'ious, haughty, proud, overbearing.

tart, sour, disagreeable.

urban'ity, courtesy, politeness, agreeableness of manner.

CARE should be taken to cultivate, in all intercourse with friends, gentle and obliging manners. It is a common error to suppose, that familiar intimacy supersedes attention to the lesser duties of behaviour; and that, under the notion of freedom, it may excuse a careless, or even a rough demeanour. On the contrary, an intimate connexion can only be perpetuated by a constant endeavour to be pleasing and agreeable. The same behaviour which procures friendship, is absolutely necessary to the preservation of it.

Let no harshness, no appearance of neglect, no supercilious affectation of superiority, be encouraged in the intercourse of friends. A tart reply, a proneness to rebuke, a captious and contradictory spirit, are often known to embitter domestic life, and to set friends at variance; it is only by continuing courtesy, and urbanity of behaviour, that we long preserve the comforts of friendship.

You must often have observed, that nothing is so strong a recommendation, on a slight acquaintance, as politeness; nor does it lose its value by time or intimacy, when preserved, as it ought to be, in the nearest connexions and strictest friendships.

In general, propriety of behaviour must be the fruit of instruction, of observation, and of reasoning; and it is to be cultivated and improved like any other branch of knowledge or virtue. Particular modes and ceremonies of behaviour vary in different places. These can only be learned by observation on the manners of those who are best skilled in them. But the principles of politeness are the same in all places. Wherever there are human beings, it must be impolitic to hurt the temper or pain the feelings of those you converse with. By raising people up, instead of mortifying and depressing them, we make ourselves so many friends, in place of enemies.

The Two Hughs

Up to this, Ulster had enjoyed a certain amount of freedom from attack. It was now the last stronghold of Irish customs and way of life. But as the rest of the country was brought into subjection, it was clear that an attack on Ulster would not be long delayed.

The Irish resistance in the North found two great leaders—the two Hughs, Hugh O'Neill and Hugh O'Donnell.

Hugh O'Neill (Aodh Ó Néill)

Hugh O'Neill was the son of Matthew, the half-brother and rival of Shane. When his father was killed, Hugh was only a little boy. He was taken to London by the English and was brought up in the house of a nobleman, where he was educated and trained as a soldier. He often visited Elizabeth's court and was a great favourite there.

O'Neill prepares for war

Hugh was given the title " Earl of Tyrone," and the English hoped that he would be a " Queen's O'Neill " and that he would oppose the " Irish O'Neill," thus dividing and weakening his people in Ulster.

But when Hugh grew up and returned home, he was so popular with his people that they made him their chief.

Wiser than his uncle Shane, he made peace and friendship with his neighbours, the O'Donnells and MacDonnells. Knowing that war could not be long delayed, he trained his men and laid in stores of food and ammunition.

Red Hugh (Aodh Rua)

Red Hugh O'Donnell was the son of the chief of Tír Chonaill. At fifteen he was a lad of great promise, and so the English determined to get hold of him. They kidnapped him and imprisoned him in Dublin Castle.

Red Hugh spent four years in prison. Then he escaped, and after enduring much hardship, he managed to reach home at last. He was welcomed by his people and on the death of his father he was made chief of his clan.

Such were the two men who were to lead the Irish in the last stand of the native chiefs against the foreigner.

THINGS TO DO

1. Find Tír Chonaill and Tyrone on the map.
2. Tell what you know of Hugh O'Neill and of Red Hugh O'Donnell.

Red Hugh comes home after four years' imprisonment.

ÓRÓ, 'SÉ DO BHEATHA 'BHAILE!

Curfá:
Óró! 'sé do bheatha 'bhaile!
Óró! 'sé do bheatha 'bhaile!
Óró! 'sé do bheatha 'bhaile!
Anois ar theacht an tsamhraidh.

'Sé do bheatha! a bhean ba léanmhar!
B'é ár gcreach tú bheith i ngéibheann,
Do dhúiche bhreá i seilbh méirleach
'S tú díolta leis na Gallaibh.
Curfá

Tá Gráinne Mhaol ag teacht thar sáile,
Óglaigh armtha léi mar gharda;
Gaeil iad féin 's ní Gaill ná Spáinnigh,
'S cuirfid ruaig ar Ghallaibh.
Curfá

A bhuí le Rí na bhFeart go bhfeiceam,
Muna mbeam beo 'na dhiaidh ach seachtain,
Gráinne Mhaol agus míle gaiscíoch
Ag fógairt fáin ar Ghallaibh.
Curfá

Pádraig Mac Piarais (1879–1916)

SHOP BILLS

(1)

> CORNER STORES,
>> HIGH STREET,
>>> MONEYTOWN
>
> Date...........
>
> Name of Customer
>
>> ....
>
> Bought of
>
>> THOMAS O'GRADY
>>> GROCER

Jan. 15   £   s.   d.
2 loaves bread @ 6¼d. each   ..
¼ lb. tea @ 2s. 8d. per lb.   ..
½ doz. eggs @ 3s. 6d. a doz.   ..
2 lbs. butter @ 2s. 8d. per lb.   ..
½ doz. boxes of matches @ 1½d.
    each   ..   ..   ..

(2) Make out the following bills:

> 1½ lb. suet @ 1s. 2d. per lb.
>
> 3½ lbs. sirloin @ 2s. 6d. per lb.
>
> 4¼ lbs. leg of lamb @ 3s. 0d. per lb.
>
> 5 lbs. corned beef @ 1s. 10d. per lb.
>
> 1½ lb. steak @ 2s. 8d. per lb.

(3) $2\frac{1}{2}$ lbs. butter @ 2s. 8d. per lb.
           2 lbs. margarine @ 1s. 9d. per lb.
           $\frac{1}{2}$ lb. cheese @ 2s. 1d. per lb.
           2 tins sardines @ 1s. 7d. each.
           1 bottle sauce @ 11d.

(4) $\frac{1}{2}$ doz. egg-cups @ $5\frac{1}{2}$d. each.
           2 jugs @ 2s. 11d. each.
           $\frac{1}{2}$ doz. tea-plates @ 1s. 3d. each.
           4 dinner-plates @ 2s. 2d. each.
           $\frac{1}{2}$ doz. tumblers @ $10\frac{1}{2}$d. each.

(5)   2 lbs. rice @ 10d. per lb.
           4 jellies @ 9d. each.
           2 lbs. sultanas @ 1s. 2d. per lb.
           $\frac{1}{2}$ lb. currants @ 1s. 3d. per lb.
           2 packets peas @ 11d. each.

(6)   3 lbs. tomatoes @ 2s. 4d. per lb.
           $2\frac{1}{2}$ lbs. oranges @ 9d. per lb.
           3 lemons @ $4\frac{1}{2}$d. each.
           2 lbs. apples @ 1s. 4d. per lb.
           3 lbs. plums @ 1s. 9d. per lb.

(7) $\frac{1}{2}$ stone strawberries @ 1/6 per lb.
           $\frac{1}{2}$ stone raspberries @ 1/3 per lb.
           10 lbs. loganberries @ 1/4 per lb.
           1 stone blackcurrants @ 1/2 per lb.

(8) Dairy for **1** month :
  152 pints milk @ **4½**d. per pt.
  8½ doz. eggs @ **3/6** a doz.

(9) Hotel bill for family of **3** adults :
  3 bed and breakfast @ **12/6**
  3 dinners   @ **4/6**
  3 teas   @ **2/6**

(10) **30** canes @ **2/9** per doz.
 2 doz. flower-pots @ **5/3** per doz.
 1 watering can @ **14/6**
 1 wheel-barrow @ **47/–**

(11) June 2.   Bread **10¾**d. Oranges **2/8**. Flour **1/–**.
   June 3.   Bread **10¾**d. Potatoes **11**d.
        Butter **2/8**.
   June 4.   Bread **1/0½**. Currants **1/3**.
        Matches **1/6**.
   June 5.   Bread **10¾**d. Rashers **1/8**.
        Sugar **1/1½**.

(12)   ¼ stone flake-meal @ **7/–** per stone.
    3 loaves bread @ **6¼**d. each.
    3 lbs. butter @ **2/8** per lb.
    ½ stone potatoes @ **1/9** per stone.

(13)   **3** pkts. soap powder @ **7**d. each.
    ¼ stone washing soda @ **3**d. per lb.
    2 pots jam @ **1/5½** each.
    ½ doz. eggs @ **3/6** per doz.

mola, *a mill for grinding,* as molar.

moveo (*motus*), *I move,* as emotion, remove.

multus, *many,* as multitude.

munus, *a gift,* and **facio,** *I do* or *make,* as munificence.

musa, *a song,* as music.

muto, *I change,* as mutation.

narro, *I relate* or *tell,* as narrative.

natus, *born,* as native.

navis, *a ship,* as navy, navigate.

necto (*nexus*), *I tie, I bind,* as connect.

negotium, *business,* as negotiate.

nihil, *nothing,* as annihilate.

norma, *a rule,* as enormous.

nosco (*notus*), *I know,* as ignorant.

numerus, *number,* as enumerate.

nuntio, *I tell,* as announce.

obscurus, *dark,* as obscurity.

opes, *riches, wealth,* as opulent.

opto, *I choose, I wish,* as adopt.

opus (*operis*), *a work,* as operation.

ordo (*ordinis*), *order,* and **extra,** *beyond,* as extraordinary.

origo (*originis*), *the origin* or *beginning,* as origin, original.

orior, *I rise,* **oriens,** *rising,* as oriental.

oro (*oratus*), *I pray,* as orator, adore.

ostendo, *I show,* as ostensible.

pando (*pansus*), *I spread,* as expand, expanse.

par, *equal,* as compeer.

pars (*partis*), *a part,* as partial.

pasco, *I feed,* **pastus,** *fed,* as pasture.

pater, *a father,* **patria,** *one's native land,* as patrimony.

patior (*passus*), *I suffer,* as patience, passion.

pello (*pulsus*), *I drive,* as expel, compulsion.

pendeo, *I hang down,* as suspend.

pendo (*pensus*), *I pay,* as compensation, expense.

peragro, *I travel about, wander* (from **per,** *through,* and **ager,** *a field*): hence pilgrim through the Italian.

pes (*pedis*), *the foot,* as impediment.

peto (*petitus*), *I seek,* as appetite.

pingo (*pictus*), *I paint,* as depict, picture.

placeo (*placitus*), *I please,* as placid.

plaudo, *I clap hands,* as plaudit, applause.

plecto (*plexus*), *I bend, I twist,* as complexion, perplex.

pleo, *I fill,* as complete, accomplish.

plico, *I fold,* as implicit.

ploro, *I weep, I bewail,* as implore.

pondus (*ponderis*), *weight,* as ponderous.

pono (*positus*), *I place,* as opponent, position.

populus, *the people,* as popular.

porto, *I bear* or *carry,* as importance, report.

posse, *to be able,* as possible.

prehendo, *I seize, I lay hold of,* as apprehend.

premo (*pressus*), *I press,* as expression, depress.

primus, *first,* and **capio,** *I take,* as principal.

probo, *I prove, I try,* as probable.

prodigium, *wonder,* as prodigious.

prope, *near,* **proximus,** *nearest,* as approximate.

pungo (*punctus*), *I point,* as punctual.

punio (*punitus*), *I punish*, as punishment, impunity.

puto, *I think*, as impute.

qualis, *of what kind*, as quality.

quantus, *how much*, as quantity.

quatuor, *four*, and pes (*pedis*), *a foot*, as quadruped.

rapidus, *swift*, as rapidity.

rapio (*raptus*), *I snatch*, as rapture.

rarus, *thin*, as rarity, rarefy.

ratus, *confirmed*, as ratify.

regula, *a rule*, as regular, regulation.

reor (*ratus*), *I think*, *I judge*, as rational.

repo, *I creep*, as reptile.

res, *a thing*, as reality.

rex (*regis*), *a king*, as regal.

robur (*roboris*), *strength*, as robust.

rodo, *I gnaw*, as corrode.

rogo, *I ask*, rogatus, *asked*, as derogatory.

rota, *a wheel*, as rotation.

ruber, *red*, as ruby.

rumen, *the cud*, as ruminate.

rumpo, *I break*, ruptus, *broken*, as interrupt.

ruo, *I rush headlong, I fall down*, as ruin.

rus (*ruris*), *the country*, as rustic, rural.

sacer, *sacred*, as sacrifice.

sanctus, *holy*, as sanctify.

satis, *enough*, as sated, satisfy.

scando, *I climb*, as ascend.

scio, *I know*, as science, conscience.

scribo, *I write*, as describe.

seco (*sectus*), *I cut*, as section.

sedeo (*sessus*), *I sit*, as subside, session.

senex, *an old man*, as senate.

sentio (*sensus*), *I feel*, as sensible, sentence.

sepelio, *I bury*, sepultus, *buried*, as sepulchre.

sequor, *I follow*, secutus, *followed*, as consequence, prosecute.

serra, *a saw*, as serrated.

servio, *I serve*, as service, serf.

servo, *I keep*, as observe, preserve.

signum, *a mark*, *a sign*, as signify.

similis, *like*, as similar.

sine, *without*, and plico, *I fold*, as simple.

sisto, *I stop*, as resist.

socius, *a companion*, as social, society.

solidus, *firm*, as consolidate.

solus, *alone*, as solitary.

solvo, *I loose*, solutus, *loosed*, as dissolve, solution.

sonus, *a sound*, as sonorous.

spargo (*sparsus*), *I scatter*, as intersperse.

specio, *I see*, spectus, *seen*, as aspect.

spiro (*spiratus*), *I breathe*, as aspire, respiration.

splendeo, *I shine*, as splendour.

stipula, *a straw*, as stipulate.

struo, *I build*, structus, *built*, as structure.

suadeo (*suasus*), *I persuade*, as persuasion.

sumo, *I take*, sumptus, *taken*, as consumption.

summus, *the highest*, as summit.

surgo, *I rise*, as surge.

taberna, *a tent*, as tabernacle.

tango (*tactus*), *I touch*, as contact.

tego (*tectus*), *I cover*, as protect.

tempus (*temporis*), *time*, as temporary.

tendo, *I stretch*, as attention, extend.

tenso, *I hold*, as maintain, tenant.

tento, *I try*, as attempt, tempting.

terminus, *a boundary*, as terminate.

terra, *the earth*, as terrestrial.

testis, *a witness*, as testify, contest.

texo, *I weave*, as texture.

timeo, *I fear*, as timid

traho (*tractus*), *I draw*, as extract, contrast.

tremo, *I tremble*, as tromble, tremulous.

tribuo, *I give, I bestow*, as distribute, tributary.

turba, *a crowd*, as turbulent.

turbidus, *thick, muddy*, as turbid.

unda, *a wave*, as undulate, abound.

unus, *one*, as unite.

urbs, *a city*, as urbanity, suburb.

utilis, *useful*, as utility.

utor (*usus*), *I use*, as abuse, utensil

vado, *I go*, as evade, invasion.

vagor, *I wander*, as vagrant.

valeo, *I am strong*, as prevail.

vanus, *vain, empty*, as vain, vanity.

vapor, *vapour, steam*, as vapour, evaporate.

veho (*vectus*), *I carry*, as convey, vexation.

veneror, *I reverence, I venerate*, as venerable.

ventus, *the wind*, as ventilate.

verbum, *a word*, as verbal.

verto (*versus*), *I turn*, as inadvertent, converse.

verus, *true*, as veritable.

vestigium, *a trace*, as vestige.

vestis, *a garment*, as vestment, invest.

via, *a way*, and tres, *three*, as trivial.

video (*visus*), *I see*, as visible.

vigil, *watchful*, as vigilant.

vigor, *strength*, as vigorous, invigorate.

vinco (*victus*), *I conquer*, as victory.

vindex, *a defender*, as vindicate.

viridis, *green*, ver, *the springtime*, as verdant, vernal.

vitium, *vice*, as vitiate.

vito, *I shun, I avoid*, and in, *not*, as inevitable.

vivo (*victus*), *I live*, as vivid, victuals.

voco, *I call*, as invoke.

volo, *I will, or wish*, and bene, *well*, as benevolent.

volvo (*volutes*), *I roll*, as revolve, convulsion.

voro, *I devour*, as voracious.

vulgus, *the common people*, as vulgar.

GREEK ROOTS.

agon, *a contest or struggle*, as agony, antagonist.

allos, *another*, allellon, *of one another*, as parallel.

anthropos, *a man*, as philanthropist.

arche, *beginning, government*, as monarchy.

aristos, *the best,* and **kratos,** *power, government,* as aristocracy.

arktos, *a bear,* as arctic.

astron, *a star,* as astronomy, disaster.

atmos, *vapour, breath,* as atmosphere.

baros, *weight,* and **metron,** a *measure,* as barometer.

bios, *life,* as biography, amphibious.

chole, *bile* or *anger,* and **melan,** *black,* as melancholy.

chrusos, *gold,* as chrysalis.

elegos, *a funeral song,* as elegy.

eremos, *a desert, a solitary place,* as hermit.

ergon, *a work,* as energy.

ge, *the earth,* as geography geology.

grapho, *I write,* as graphic, geography.

gramma, *a letter,* as grammar, programme.

hodos, *a way,* as periodical, method.

konops, *a gnat, a mosquito,* as canopy, a covering over head to keep off mosquitoes.

kruos, *ice,* as crystal.

kuklos, *a circle,* as cycle.

leipo (*leipso*), *I leave out,* as eclipse, ellipsis.

logos, *a word, a discourse, reason, science,* as analogy, dialogue, catalogue.

mathema, *learning,* as mathematics.

meter, *a mother,* and **polis,** *a city,* as metropolis.

metron, *a measure,* as diameter, symmetry, thermometer.

micros, *small,* as microscope.

monos, *alone or single,* as monarch, monastic.

murios, *ten thousand,* as myriad.

oikos, *a house,* as economy.

onoma, *a name,* as anonymous.

organon, *an instrument,* as organ, organic.

oxus, *sharp,* as oxygen.

pathos, *feeling,* as sympathy.

phemi, *I speak,* as prophet.

philos, *one who loves,* as philosophy, philanthropist.

phusis, *nature,* as physical, physiology.

pneuma (*pneumatos*), *air, breath,* as pneumonia, pneumatics.

polis, *a city,* as politics, metropolis.

pur, *fire,* as pyramid.

schema, *a plan, a design,* as scheme.

skene, *a tent, the stage,* as scenery, scene.

skopeo, *I view,* as microscope, telescope.

sphaira, *a globe,* as sphere, atmosphere, hemisphere.

stasis, *a standing,* as apostasy.

stello, *I send,* as apostle, epistle.

stratos, *an army,* as stratagem.

strophe, *a turning,* as catastrophe.

taphos, *a tomb,* as epitaph.

techne, *art,* as technical.

tele, *afar,* as telescope.

therme, *heat,* as thermometer.

tome, *a cutting,* and **a,** *not* or *without,* as atom—an indivisible particle of matter.

tupos, *a work, an impression,* as type, typical.

turannos, *a king or ruler who was supposed to have enslaved his countrymen by usurping supreme power,* as tyrant, tyranny.

THE LITTLE LORD JESUS

Away in a manger, no crib for a bed,
The little Lord Jesus lay down His sweet head.
The stars in the bright sky looked down where
    He lay—
The little Lord Jesus asleep in the hay.

The cattle are lowing, the baby awakes,
But the little Lord Jesus, no crying He makes.
I love Thee, Lord Jesus! Look down from the
    sky,
And stay by my cradle till morning is nigh.

Be near me, Lord Jesus. I ask Thee to stay
Close by me for ever, and love me, I pray;
Bless all the dear children in Thy tender care,
And fit us for heaven, to live with Thee there.

THE PIPER CHARMS THE RATS

Into the street the Piper stepped,
  Smiling first a little smile,
As if he knew what magic slept
  In his quiet pipe the while;
Then, like a musical adept,
To blow the pipe his lips he wrinkled,
And green and blue his sharp eyes twinkled,
Like a candle-flame where salt is sprinkled;
And ere three shrill notes the pipe uttered,
You heard as if an army muttered;
And the muttering grew to a grumbling;
And the grumbling grew to a mighty rumbling;
And out of the houses the rats came tumbling—
Great rats, small rats, lean rats, brawny rats,
Brown rats, black rats, grey rats, tawny rats,
Grave old plodders, gay young friskers,
  Fathers, mothers, uncles, cousins,
Cocking tails and pricking whiskers,
  Families by tens and dozens,
Brothers, sisters, husbands, wives—
Followed the Piper for their lives.
From street to street he piped, advancing,
And step for step they followed, dancing.

ROBERT BROWNING—*The Pied Piper of Hamelin.*

EXERCISE 31

Unitary Method—II

(1) If a distance of **1** mile is represented by **6** inches, what distance in feet is represented by $1\frac{1}{4}$ inches. (**5,280** feet = **1** mile.)

(2) **224** gallons of water weigh **1** ton. Find the weight of water in cwt. in a full **35**-gal. tank. (**2,240** lb. = **1** ton.)

(3) A fruit-grower got **21**s. for a stone of raspberries. What was the value of **127** lb. at this rate ?

(4) What is the area of **70**% of a farm, if **20**% of it is **8** ac. **3** rds. **24** sq. per. ?

(5) Travelling at the rate of **88** yds. in **3** seconds, (a) How many yards will a train travel in one minute ? (b) What is its speed in miles per hour ?

(6) Grass-seed mixture sown at the rate of **60** lb. per Irish acre cost **130**s. for **1** acre. It would take **40** lb. of this seed to sow a statute acre. What would that cost at the same rate ?

(7) A clock shows **12.5** at noon on Monday and **12.17** at noon on Tuesday. At this rate how many minutes fast will it be at **6** p.m. (correct time) on Wednesday ?

(8) Half a ton of potatoes can be bought for £5 **12**s. **6**d. How many cwt. can be bought for £13 **10**s. **0**d. at this rate ?

(9) **12** yards of carpet cost £13 **16**s. **0**d. How many yards of the same carpet can be bought for £19 **11**s. **0**d. ?

(10) A sheet of glass **2** ft. by **1** ft. **6** in. weighs **3** lb. **12** oz. What weight of this glass is there in a partition containing **120** sq. ft. of it ? (Answer in cwt., etc.)

(11) If ·65 of a farm is worth £728, what is the value of the whole farm ?

(12) If I pay £2 5s. 0d. for the loan of £50 for a year,
    (a) What would I pay for the loan of £450 for a year at the same rate ?
    (b) What would I pay for a loan of £450 for 3½ years at the same rate ?

(13) A builder calculates that it will take 20 men 30 days to clear and level a housing site. If he puts on 25 men from the start, how long should they take to do the work ?

(14) There are 4 boys in a camp and they have a store of food for x days.
    (i) What stands for the number of days that the food would last 1 boy ?
    (ii) What stands for the number of days that the food would last y boys ?

(15) There were 117 men in a turf camp. They had a quantity of provisions to last them for 10 days when 78 extra workers arrived. How long will the provisions last ?

(16) If 270 men have enough food to last them for a fortnight, how many men must be sent away so that the food may last 4 days longer ?

(17) 525 soldiers had provisions for 21 days. When they were joined by others, the provisions lasted only 15 days. How many extra soldiers arrived ?

(18) A joint of beef weighing 3 lb. 15 oz. cost 10s. 6d. What was the weight of a joint costing 14s. 10d. at the same price per lb. ?

(19) Find the cost of 3 tons 17 cwt. of potatoes if the cost of 2 tons 9 cwt. of them was £28 3s. 6d. ?

MY BIRTH-DAY.

hap'ly, perhaps.
in'cense, odour of spices burned
  in religious rites or ceremonies.

shrines, altars.
efface, to wipe or blot out.

" My Birth-day "—what a different sound
  That word had in my youthful ears! .
And how, each time the day comes round,
  Less and less white its mark appears.

When first our scanty years are told,
  It seems like pastime to grow old;
And as Youth counts the shining links,
  That Time around him binds so fast
Pleased with the task he little thinks
  How hard that chain will press at last.

Vain was the man and false as vain,
  Who said, " were he ordained to run
His long career of life again,
  He would do all that he *had* done."
Ah, 'tis not thus the voice that dwells
  In sober birth-days, speaks to me ;
Far otherwise—of time it tells,
  Lavished unwisely, carelessly ;
Of counsel mocked ; of talents, made
  Haply for high and pure designs,
But oft, like Israel's incense, laid
  Upon unholy, earthly shrines.
All this it tells, and, could I trace
  The imperfect picture o'er again,
With power to add, retouch, efface,
  The lights and shades, the joy and pain,
How little of the past would stay !
  How quickly all should melt away—
All—but that Freedom of the Mind,
  Which hath been more than wealth to me ;
Those friendships, in my boyhood twined,
  And kept till now unchangingly ;
And that dear home, that saving ark,
  Where Love's true light at last I've found,
Cheering within, when all grows dark,
  And comfortless, and stormy round !

Thomas Moore.

íosagán

bí sean-Maitias ina ṡuí le hais a ḋorais. An té ġaḃfaḋ an bótar, ṡílfeaḋ sé gur ḋealḃ cloiċe nó marmair a ḃí ann—sin nó ḋuine marḃ—mar ní ċreiḋfeaḋ sé go ḃféaḋfaḋ fear beo fanaċt coṁ ciúin, coṁ socair sin. Ḃí a ċeann cromṫa aige agus cluas air ag éisteaċt.

Is mó sin fuaim ċeolṁar a ḃí le cloisteáil, an té a mbeaḋ aird aige ortu. Cuala sean-Maitias olagón na ḋtonn ar na carraigreaċa agus monabar an tsruiṫleáin ag sileaḋ leis an gclocar. Cuala sé scréaċ na coirre éisc ón ḋuirling, agus géimneaċ na mbó ón mbuaile, agus geal-ġáire na bpáistí ón ḃfaiċe. Aċ ní le ceaċtar acu seo a ḃí sé ag éisteaċt coṁ haireaċ sin—cé go mba binn leis iad go léir—aċ le glór glé glinn cloig an Aifrinn a ḃí ag teaċt cuige le gaoiṫ i gciúnas na maiḋne.

Ḃí na ḋaoine ar fad bailiṫe leo cuig an Aifreann. Conaic sean-Maitias ag gaḃáil tairis iad, ina nḋuine is ina nḋuine, nó ina mion-ḋreamannaiḃ. Ḃí na gearr-ḃodaiġ ag riṫ agus ag léimneaċ. Ḃí na cailíní ag sioscaḋ cainte go meiḋreaċ. Ḃí na mná ag coṁrá os íseal. Ḃí na fir ina ḋtost.

Mar sin a triallaidís an bótar gac Domnac.
Mar sin a suíod sean-Maitias ar a cataoir
ag breatnú ortu nó go dtéidís as amarc.
Triall siad tairis an maidin áirite seo mar
ba gnátac. D'fan an sean-fear ag féacaint
ortu go dtí go raib críoc leis an ngleo is leis
an bfotram, go dtí gur glan an plód deir-
eannac barr ardáin na cille, go dtí nac raib
le feiceáil ac bótar fada díreac ag sínead
amac is é bán, go dtí nac raib fágta ar an
mbaile ac corr-sean-duine ina leaba, na páistí
ag cleasaíoct ar an bfaice, agus é féin ina
suí le hais a dorais.

ON THE LEE.

We live near the Lee, a few miles from Cork, and spend much time in our boat on the river.

Dad brings his rod and line to fish for trout, while I steer the boat as it glides down the stream past woods and hill-sides.

It is like a scene from Tír na nÓg, all green and golden, when the sun shines on the waters.

I.W. BEG. BK.

8 A. Read this: then answer the questions which follow :

A DAY ON THE BOG

The sun had not yet risen when I heard Father calling me. I washed and dressed quickly, said my prayers and ate a hurried meal under the impatient eye of Father. He had already finished breakfast and had harnessed the donkey in readiness for an early start. I gulped down my meal, picked up the food-basket and climbed into the donkey-cart beside him.

The sun had barely risen when we reached the bog, but already men were hard at work, plying turf-spades, wheeling barrows laden with fresh turf, or setting wet sods on end to dry.

The sun shone in the clear morning sky. Larks sang high above us. Bees hummed. The bog-cotton fluttered in the light breeze. Blue hills ringed the flat brown bog. But Father gave me little time to enjoy these pleasant things. He promptly set me to work lifting the heavy sods as he cut them out of the soft bank.

About mid-day, to my great joy, he ordered me to get a meal ready. I made a fire of pieces of bog-wood and dry scraps of turf, and set the kettle to boil. The tea tasted a little of turf-smoke, but I found it altogether delicious. When not a scrap of food was left in the basket, I lay on my back and watched the larks soaring and dropping in the clear air. Too soon Father ordered me back to work.

It was a long day and a hard day, but it was a happy day, too. I ate an enormous supper that night and slept like a log.

Questions

1. Why, do you think, was the boy's father impatient to start ?
2. How did the boy and his father go to the bog ?
3. What work were the men doing on the bog ?

4. What pleasant things could be seen on the bog ?
5. What work was the boy set to do ?
6. Of what did the boy make the fire ?
7. Why, do you think, did the boy find the tea so delicious ?
8. Explain these words : bog, donkey, gulped, barely.
9. What part of speech is each word in the following sentences ?. State the kind, number and case of the nouns and pronouns : (a) The sun shone in the clear sky. (b) Swarms of bees hummed about us. (c) Tom watched the larks which soared and sang in the clear air.
10. Analyse the following sentences : (a) The boy dressed himself quickly. (b) The man wheeled the dry turf across the bog.

B. Composition : A day spent working in the garden, *or* gathering blackberries, *or* at the seaside.

C. KINDS OF ADJECTIVES
The main classes of adjectives are—

1. Descriptive adjectives
These are adjectives which describe persons or things : a *happy* holiday, a *windy* night, a *tall* boy, a *blue* dress. Most adjectives belong to this class.

2. Possessive adjectives
These adjectives show possession or ownership. They are *my, thy, your, his, her, our, their, its.*

3. Demonstrative adjectives
These point out the noun to which they refer : *this* hat, *that* man, *these* pens, *those* children.

4. Interrogative adjectives
These ask questions : *What* answer did you give ? *Which* way did he go ? I asked him *what* plans he had made.

Remember that when these words go with nouns, they are interrogative adjectives : when they stand alone, they are interrogative pronouns.

5. Adjectives of Number and Quantity

Under this heading come

(a) Cardinal Numerals : *one* man, *two* men, etc.

(b) Ordinal Numerals : the *first* man, *second* class, etc.

(c) A number of adjectives which indicate quantity or number : *some* things, *both* boys, *many* girls, *few* men.

Note that when these words go with nouns, they are adjectives : when they stand alone, they are pronouns.

Many people came but *few* people stayed. (Adjectives.)

Many are called but *few* are chosen. (Pronouns.)

A, an, the: These words point out nouns and are, therefore, demonstrative adjectives. Generally, however, they are called **Articles**. *The* is the **Definite Article**. *A* or *an* is an **Indefinite Article**.

D. Pick out the adjectives in the following sentences: state what kind of adjective each is:

1. Great rats, small rats, lean rats, brawny rats,
   Brown rats, black rats, grey rats, tawny rats,
   Grave old plodders, gay young friskers.

2. She is not a beautiful woman : she is short and stout ; she wears thick shoes and a plain dress with a little shawl and an old-fashioned bonnet ; but there is determination in her calm face and her eyes are the eyes of a mother.

E. Say whether the words in italics are adjectives or pronouns:

1. Give me *that* book : leave *this* where it is. 2. *This* pen is better than *that*. 3. *One* day you will be *one* of the world's workers. 4. *Both* boys passed the examination and *both* received prizes. 5. *Some* people are happy and *some* are miserable. 6. *Her* exercise is good : *his* is not good. 7. *All* articles in the shop are for sale. 8. *This* competition is open to *all*. 9. *Which* pen is *yours* ?

BELLING THE CAT

The mice held a meeting one night. They wanted to think out some way of keeping themselves safe from the cat.

They sat round in a circle and looked very worried indeed. Not one of them could think of a plan.

Then young Short-Whiskers spoke up. "Why are you all so worried?" he said. "The thing is simple."

"Simple!" said one of the old mice. "How do you make that out?"

"Our trouble is that we cannot hear the cat coming," said Short-Whiskers.

"Agreed!" said the old mouse.

"Well," said Short-Whiskers, "all we have to do is to get a small bell and tie it round the cat's neck with a ribbon. Then, when we hear the bell tinkling, we shall know that the cat is about."

When the mice heard this plan, they clapped their paws with joy.

"Splendid!" said one young mouse. "I think a silver bell would be best."

"No," cried another. "A little brass bell would be the very thing."

One of the mother mice said that the bell should have a red ribbon, and another said she felt sure that a blue one would be better.

The talk went on and on for fully ten minutes. Then old Grey-Whiskers stood up on his hind legs. He was the oldest mouse in the house—and the wisest—so all the others listened carefully.

"There is only one thing wrong with this splendid plan," he said. "Who is going to tie the bell on the cat's neck?"

All the mice looked at one another then, but none of them spoke. Grey-Whiskers looked straight at young Short-Whiskers, but Short-Whiskers had nothing to say either. He was afraid that he might be asked to bell the cat himself, so he lowered his eyes and made himself as small as he could.

"It seems," said Grey-Whiskers then, "that nobody is going to bell the cat. In that case, our meeting is over, and I am going to bed."

Off to bed he went then, and very soon all the other mice followed him one by one.

1. The mice sat in a line. Was it a straight line or a curved one?

2. What did the mice do when Short-Whiskers had finished speaking?

3. What question did Grey-Whiskers ask?

4. Why did Short-Whiskers not offer to bell the cat?

abcdefghijklmnopqrstuvwxyz

abcdefghijklmnopqrstuvwxyz

LOOP JOINS :

for float, boat before fury foot foof

roar roor very good ten noon

maff and fran a very fine effort

fer, fir, fo, fum

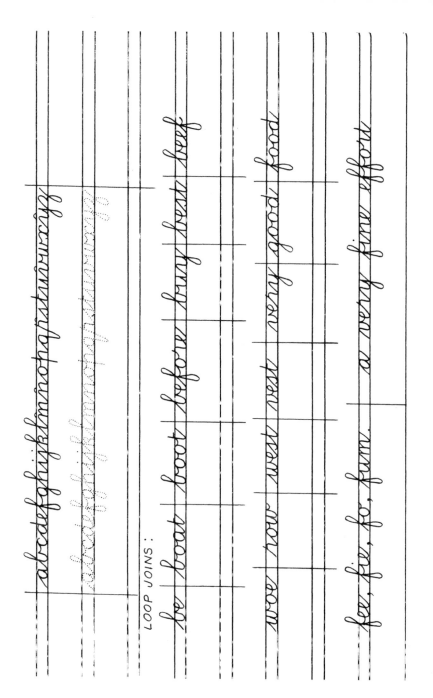

113

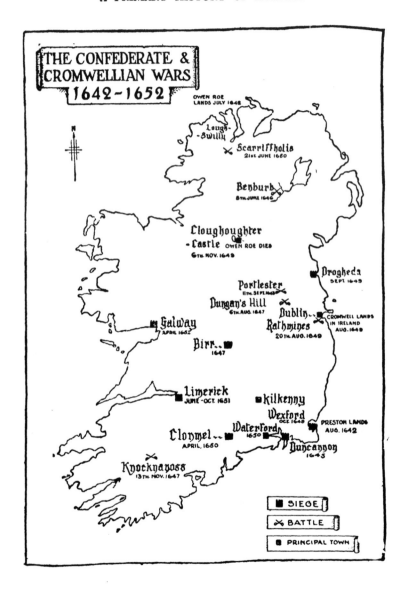

THE CONFEDERATE &
CROMWELLIAN WARS
1642~1652

OWEN ROE
LANDS JULY 1642

Lough
-Swilly

Scarriffholis
21st JUNE 1650

Benburb
8TH JUNE 1646

Cloughoughter
-Castle OWEN ROE DIES
6TH. NOV. 1649

Drogheda
SEPT. 1649

Portlester
11TH. SEPT. 1643

Dungan's Hill
6TH. AUG. 1647

Dublin

Rathmines
20TH. AUG. 1649

CROMWELL LANDS
IN IRELAND
AUG. 1649

Galway
APRIL 1652

Birr
1647

Limerick
JUNE -OCT. 1651

Kilkenny

Wexford
OCT. 1649

PRESTON LANDS
AUG. 1642

Clonmel
APRIL 1650

Waterford
1650

Duncannon
1645

Knocknanoss
13TH. NOV. 1647

■ SIEGE

✕ BATTLE

⊟ PRINCIPAL TOWN

Cromwell

King Charles I was defeated and put to death by his people. England then became a republic, or commonwealth, under Oliver Cromwell.

The people of Ireland were shocked at the killing of the king. All parties in the country disliked the new government of England. Cromwell feared that Ireland would be used as a base for attacks on the new republic. He came over with a large army.

Oliver Cromwell

Cromwell was a man of iron will. He was stern and without pity. He spent only nine months in Ireland, but he left a name that has never been forgotten. He believed that the Irish had killed thousands of helpless " planters " in Ulster. He considered that he had a mission to punish them.

Cromwell's soldiers were so well drilled and disciplined that they were known as *Ironsides*. His heavy guns were the largest and best made at the time.

Death of Eoghan Rua

Eoghan Rua had kept his army together. He was the only man who might have opposed Cromwell with any chance of success. But Eoghan Rua died soon after Cromwell's coming to Ireland. The country was worn out after eight years of war. The people were without a leader.

Drogheda

Cromwell landed at Ringsend. Dublin was held by his own forces, so he went at once to Drogheda which was held by the forces of the king.

Cromwell's big guns soon tore through the walls of Drogheda. Then his men killed every person they found in the town. Not only the soldiers—many of whom were Englishmen—but priests, old men, women and even children were killed in cold blood.

Writing to England from Drogheda, Cromwell described how 2,000 people were slaughtered, and added: " I am persuaded that this is a righteous judgement of God upon those barbarous wretches, who have imbrued their hands in so much innocent blood."

After the massacre of Drogheda, a number of northern towns surrendered to Cromwell.

Wexford

Cromwell then went to Wexford. There the same thing happened. The town was taken : men, women and children were killed without mercy.

Cromwell reckoned that after two such examples of his ruthlessness, the other towns would give him little trouble. In the next few months he took nearly all the chief towns of Leinster and Munster.

Clonmel

Clonmel was defended by a small garrison under Hugh Dubh O'Neill, a nephew of Eoghan Rua. There Cromwell met a well-planned resistance and lost two thousand men. Hugh Dubh and his men got safely away before Cromwell could enter the town.

Cromwell then went back to England, leaving his son-in-law, Ireton, to carry on the war.

The remaining towns soon surrendered. Ireland was at the feet of the conqueror.

DATES

Death of Eoghan Rua Ó Néill—1649.
Cromwell came to Ireland—August, 1649.
Cromwell left Ireland—May, 1650.

THINGS TO DO

1. Tell what you know about Oliver Cromwell.
2. Name three O'Neills who fought gallantly for Ireland. Tell what you know of each.
3. If you live in or near Drogheda, Wexford, Youghal or Clonmel, collect as much information as you can about the happenings in your town in Cromwell's time. Write a little account of them.

THE WIND FROM THE WEST

Blow high, blow low,
    O wind from the west,
You come from the country
    I love the best.

O say have the lilies
    Yet lifted their heads
Above the lake-water
    That ripples and spreads?

Do the little sedges
　　　Still shake with delight,
And whisper together
　　　All through the night?

Have the mountains the purple
　　　I used to love,
And peace about them,
　　　Around and above?

O wind from the west,
　　　Blow high, blow low,
You come from the country
　　　I loved long ago.

ELLA YOUNG

LINES ADDRESSED TO A SEA GULL SEEN OFF THE CLIFFS OF MOHER, IN THE COUNTY OF CLARE.

GERALD GRIFFIN was born at Limerick in 1803. He commenced his literary career by writing articles for newspapers and magazines; but he soon abandoned this occupation for the composition of some very interesting tales and stories of Irish life, such as *Holland-Tide*, or *Munster Popular Festivals.* In 1829 appeared the most popular of all his works, "The Collegians," and a *second* series of *Tales of the Munster Festivals.* He is also the author of several pleasing poems. He became a Christian Brother, in Cork, in 1838 ; and in 1840 he died in that city.

bil'low, the ocean wave.
plumes, feathers.
pois'ing, balancing.
surge, a swelling wave of the sea.

cloud-curtained dome, dome or vault of the heavens, curtained by the clouds.
pin'ion, a wing.
fur'led, rolled up as a flag on its staff.

WHITE bird of the tempest ! oh, beautiful thing,
With the bosom of snow, and the motionless wing,
Now sweeping the billow, now floating on high,
Now bathing thy plumes in the light of the sky,
Now poising o'er ocean thy delicate form,
Now breasting the surge with thy bosom so warm,
Now darting aloft, with a heavenly scorn,
Now shooting along like a ray of the morn ;
Now lost in the folds of the cloud-curtained dome,
Now floating abroad like a flake of the foam ;
Now silently poised o'er the war of the main,
Like the spirit of charity brooding o'er pain ;

LINES TO A SEA GULL.

Now gliding with pinion, all silently furled,
Like an Angel descending to comfort the world.
Thou seem'st to my spirit, as upward I gaze—
And see thee, now clothed in mellowest rays,
Now lost in the storm-driven vapours that fly,
Like hosts that are routed across the broad sky—
Like a pure spirit true to its virtue and faith,
'Mid the tempests of nature, of passion, and death!
Rise! beautiful emblem of purity! rise
On the sweet winds of heaven, to thine own
  brilliant skies,
Still higher! still higher! till lost to our sight,
Thou hidest thy wings in a mantle of light;
And I think how a pure spirit gazing on thee,
Must long for the moment—the joyous and free—
When the soul, disembodied from nature, shall
  · spring,
Unfettered, at once to her Maker and King;
When the bright day of service and suffering past,
Shapes, fairer than thine, shall shine round her at
  last,
While the standard of battle triumphantly furled,
She smiles like a victor, serene on the world!

Gerald Griffin.

CHAPTER XVIII

THE FOURTH, FIFTH AND SIXTH COMMANDMENTS OF GOD

234. What is the fourth commandment of God ?

The fourth commandment of God is : Honour thy father and thy mother.

＊235. What is commanded by the fourth commandment ?

We are commanded by the fourth commandment to love, honour and obey our parents.

236. How are we to love our parents ?

We are to love our parents by wishing them well, by being kind to them in word and deed, and by helping them in their necessities.

237. How are we to honour our parents ?

We are to honour our parents by treating them always with respect, by showing gratitude to them and by bearing patiently with their faults and weaknesses.

THE HOME AT NAZARETH

238. How are we to obey our parents ?

We are to obey our parents while under their care by doing readily what they command, provided it be not sinful.

239. What are the chief duties of parents ?

The chief duties of parents are : to provide for their children, to watch over and correct them, and by instruction and good example to lead them to God.

240. Does the fourth commandment oblige us to respect and obey others besides our parents ?

Besides our parents, the fourth commandment obliges us to respect and to obey all our lawful superiors, both spiritual and temporal.

241. What are the chief duties of employers ?

The chief duties of employers are : to pay their employees a just wage, to treat them kindly as brothers in Christ, and to help them to observe their moral and religious duties.

242. What are the chief duties of employees ?

The chief duties of employees are : to work honestly, to obey the lawful commands of their employer, and to safeguard his property when committed to their care.

243. What are our chief duties as citizens ?

Our chief duties as citizens are : to love and serve our country, and to respect and obey the lawful government.

244. How do we love and serve our country ?

We love and serve our country principally by observing its laws, defending its rights, voting honestly, and paying just taxes.

245. Why should we respect and obey the lawful government ?

We should respect and obey the lawful government because its authority comes from God.

246. Is it sinful to join a society that plots against the lawful government ?

Yes ; it is a mortal sin to join a society that plots to overthrow by force or other sinful measures the lawful government.

247. What are the chief duties of those who hold public office ?

The chief duties of those who hold public office are : to be just and impartial and to promote the general welfare.

248. What is the fifth commandment of God ?

The fifth commandment of God is : Thou shalt not kill.

*249. What is forbidden by the fifth commandment ?

The fifth commandment forbids murder and suicide, and all other acts that inflict bodily injury on ourselves or on others.

*250. What else is forbidden by the fifth commandment ?

The fifth commandment also forbids drunkenness, quarrelling, anger and revenge, because they lead to injury of ourselves or of others.

251. What are they bound to do who have caused bodily injury to others ?

They who have inflicted bodily injury on others are bound to make good the loss they have caused.

252. What are we commanded by the fifth commandment?

We are commanded by the fifth commandment to take reasonable care to preserve our own life and health and to avoid causing bodily injury to others.

253. What is the sixth commandment ?

The sixth commandment is : Thou shalt not commit adultery.

254. What is the purpose of the sixth commandment ?

The purpose of the sixth commandment is to safeguard the sanctity of marriage and to maintain right conduct between men and women.

*255. What is forbidden by the sixth commandment ?

The sixth commandment forbids not only adultery, but all looks, words and actions against the virtue of chastity.

256. What are the chief dangers to chastity ?

The chief dangers to chastity are idleness, intemperance, bad companions, improper dances, immodest dress, company-keeping, and indecent conversation, books, plays and pictures.

257. What are the chief means of preserving chastity?

The chief means of preserving chastity are : to be modest in our dress and conduct, to avoid the occasion of sin, to cultivate devotion to the Blessed Virgin Mary, and above all to seek the help of God through prayer and the sacraments.

The Norsemen

About the end of the eighth century, a race of fierce fighters began to attack the coasts of Europe. They were the Norsemen, and they came from the countries now called Norway, Sweden and Denmark.

The land in these countries was poor, and as their populations increased, many people were hungry. So the boldest of them took to their boats and sailed the seas in search of plunder.

A Viking long boat.

Norse conquests

The Norsemen invaded England and forced the chief king to pay them tribute. They seized and held a part of France, which is called Normandy to this day. They plundered the coasts of Italy. They occupied the islands of Scotland and the Isle of Man.

Attacks on Ireland

The Norse raiders who attacked Ireland are called "the Danes" or "na Lochlannaigh" in the old stories, but we now know that most of them came from Norway.

Norway is a land of mountains and forests. Long arms of the sea run far inland, and in the little bays, or *viks*, the Norsemen built their long boats of stout oak. The Vikings, as these Norsemen were called, were great sailors.

Ireland was an easy country for them to attack. It has long deep bays on its coasts, and many rivers up which the raiders could row their boats. No part of the country is more than fifty miles from the sea.

THINGS TO DO

1. Find Norway, Sweden and Denmark on the map of Europe. Trace the route by which you think the Norsemen came to Ireland.
2. Find some of the countries conquered by the Norsemen.
3. Tell in your own words all you know about the Norsemen.
4. Why was Ireland an easy country for the Norsemen to attack?
5. If you have read any old Norse stories, tell them to your teacher.

an fιrín sa ɣleann

bí τιɣín sa ɣleann,
Is fιrín beaɣ cam
Ina cónaí ann
    Ina aonar.

Ní raιb aιɣe ór,
Ní raιb aιɣe stór,
Capall ná bó,
    Ná éinní.

lá ɒá ṡaol
fuaιr sé leaṫ-réal,
Is cuaιɣ sé ar aonac
    An Márta.

Ceannaιɣ sé cat
Is puιsín beaɣ breac,
Is maιrιɒ ɣo léιr
    ɣo sásta.

M.E.

130

THE HISTORY OF THE OLD TESTAMENT.

SKY, LAND, WATER, AND TREES.

1.—The Creation of the World.

The world in which we live had a beginning. Before that beginning there was no land nor sea, nor bright blue sky. There were no trees nor plants nor flowers. There was no person nor thing but God. He always was and always will be.

In the beginning God made the world, the land, and the water; the sun, the moon, and the stars; the birds and the fishes and all the creatures of the earth.

Last of all, God made a man and a woman. Adam and Eve were their names. They are called our First Parents.

And God is so great and so powerful that He made all these out of nothing, by His word alone. In the six days of creation He made everything.

On the seventh day God rested from His work, and blessed that day. For this reason the Jews kept it holy,

FISHES, BIRDS, AND LAND ANIMALS.

and called it the *Sabbath,* which means *rest from labour.* But after Our Blessed Lord was crucified by the wicked Jews the Apostles chose Sunday, the first day of the week, as their day of rest, because on that day our Saviour arose from the dead.

QUESTIONS.

1. How did God make the world?
2. Why did He bless the seventh day of the week?
3. Why do we keep the first day of the week holy instead of the seventh day?
4. Who were Adam and Eve?

1A.—The Creation and Fall of the Angels.

God also created angels. Angels cannot be seen, because they are spirits without bodies. They are God's messengers, and can travel faster than lightning. They understand things that no man can understand, and they can do things that no man can do.

At first they were all good and happy. But afterwards

THE GREAT BATTLE IN HEAVEN.

some of them sinned through pride. The leader of the bad angels was Lucifer. Then Michael and the other good angels fought against the bad angels. God made a place of punishment, called Hell, and the bad angels were driven into it. Now they are called devils, and Lucifer, the chief devil, is now known as Satan. The devils hate us and try to get us to sin so that we shall go to Hell too.

God rewarded the good angels by making them happy for ever. Some of them are sent to be our Guardian Angels. They watch over us and pray for us and keep us from harm.

QUESTIONS.

1. What else did God create?
2. Why cannot we see angels?
3. What can angels do?
4. Were all the angels good at first?
5. How did some of them become bad?
6. What became of the bad angels?
7. How did God reward the good angels?

THE GARDEN OF PARADISE.

2.—The Garden of Paradise.

The home of Adam and Eve was a lovely garden in which sweet-smelling flowers and ripe, juicy fruits grew. Pretty birds sang in the branches of the trees and animals of every kind sported and played together. Everything was peaceful and beautiful.

God told Adam that he and Eve might eat the fruit of every tree in the garden, except of one, and that one they must not touch.

QUESTIONS.
1. Where did Adam and Eve live?
2. What did God tell them that they were not to do?

3.—The First Sin.

This was a very little thing to require, and had our first parents obeyed God they would have lived for ever and would have been happy in this beautiful garden. But one day the devil tempted Eve to eat the forbidden fruit, and told her that if she ate it she would become as wise as God Himself.

ADAM AND EVE DRIVEN OUT OF THE GARDEN OF PARADISE.

Eve was foolish and wicked enough to believe this, and in spite of God's command, she ate the forbidden fruit. Then, not satisfied with sinning herself, she coaxed Adam to eat the fruit also, and in this way sin was brought upon the earth.

Almighty God was angry with Adam and Eve for disobeying Him. To punish them, He drove them from the garden, and condemned them to spend the rest of their lives in labour and suffering, until they returned to the dust out of which they were made.

This terrible curse was to fall not only on them, but on all who came after them. But so great is the love of God for His creatures, that, even in spite of their sin, He promised that He would send a Redeemer to save mankind.

QUESTIONS.

1. How did the devil persuade Eve to eat the forbidden fruit?
2. Why did Adam eat the forbidden fruit?
3. How were Adam and Eve punished?
4. What promise did God make?

A VISIT FROM THE SEA

Far from the loud sea beaches,
  Where he goes fishing and
    crying,
Here in the inland garden
  Why is the sea-gull flying?

Here are no fish to dive for;
  Here is the corn and lea;
Here are the green trees rustling,
  Hie away home to sea.

Fresh is the river water,
  And quiet among the rushes;
This is no home for the sea-gull,
  But for the rooks and thrushes,

Pity the bird that has wandered!
　　Pity the sailor ashore!
Hurry him home to the ocean,
　　Let him come here no more.

High on the sea-cliff ledges
　　The white gulls are trooping
　　　and crying,
Here among rocks and roses,
　　Why is the sea-gull flying?

R. L. STEVENSON

LABHAIR AN TEANGA GHAEILGE

Ó labhair an teanga Ghaeilge liom,
 A chuid mo chroí is a stór,
An teanga a labhair mo mháthair liom,
 In Éirinn ghlas fadó.
'Sí teanga bhinn ár sinsear í,
 An chaint is milse glór:
Ó labhair an teanga Ghaeilge liom,
 Is bain dem' chroí an brón.

Ó labhair an teanga Ghaeilge liom,
 'Sí teanga cheart na nGael:
An teanga bhinn is ársa 'tá
 Lé fáil ar fud an tsaoil.
A stór mo chroí is beannacht ort,
 A chailin óig gan cháim,
Cá bhfuil sa saol aon teanga mar
 Ár dteanga féin le fáil?

   Ní fios cé a chum

HOW HANS SAVED HARLEM

Little Hans was a Dutch boy, and he lived in the town of Harlem. Now Harlem, like many parts of Holland, is beneath the level of the sea, which is kept out by great banks of earth and stone, called dykes.

One day Hans was sent by his mother to bring some gingerbread cakes to an old friend of the family, who lived some miles away. Hans spent some time with this friend, and then set out to walk back to Harlem.

He walked on the grassy top of the dyke, from which he could see both the sea and the countryside : and as he looked down at the fields he began to think of what would happen if the dyke burst. The sea-water would pour in through the opening, carrying death to house and farm.

After walking for a mile or so, Hans sat down to rest himself. Then he heard a faint trickle of water, and, looking down on the inland side of the dyke, he saw a tiny hole, through which a small stream of water was flowing.

Hans was frightened. He knew what a leak in the dyke meant ! The tiny opening would grow bigger as the earth was carried away, until the sea burst through and swept down over houses, farms, and towns. It would cover Harlem, and the little brick house where his mother and father and his brothers and sisters were living.

Hans slid to the bottom of the dyke, and thrust his arm into the tiny hole.

" Not while I can help it shall Harlem be washed away," he said to himself.

II.

He cried for help, but no help came. He looked about for something to block the hole, but he could see nothing that would suit. His arm alone could keep out the water, and he held it there bravely.

When darkness came, and the moon rose, the sound of the waves seemed to grow louder. The waters beat on the sides of the dyke, and seemed to be trying to force the boy's tiny arm out of the hole they had made.

When Hans felt his right arm grow numb he pulled it out and put his left arm in its place. But before long, the left arm, too, grew numb, and the right arm went in again. Hans lay there in the darkness, praying that God would give him the strength to save Harlem.

Slowly the long hours passed, and then, at long last, the dawn broke. But it was several hours later before help came.

Towards six o'clock, a milkman and his son drove along the top of the dyke in a dog-cart.

"Help! Help!" cried Hans faintly. The milkman looked down over the side of the dyke.

EC

"Whatever are you doing down there at this hour of the morning?" he cried.

"There is a leak in the dyke and I am keeping the water out," said Hans simply. "Go and bring help as soon as you can."

The milkman sent his son to Harlem for help, and told Hans to stand up and stretch his cold limbs. Then he put his own arm into the hole.

Soon a crowd of men came running from the city, bringing with them shovels and sand-bags. They repaired the hole in the dyke, and they carried brave little Hans back to Harlem on their shoulders.

"Make way for the hero of Harlem!" they cried.

And to this day the people of Holland honour the memory of the noble boy who remained at his post all night through and saved the city of Harlem.

A CHILD'S EVENING PRAYER.

Jesus, tender Shepherd, hear me;
  Bless Thy little lamb to-night;
Through the darkness be Thou near me;
  Keep me safe till morning light.

All this day Thy hand has led me,
  And I thank Thee for Thy care;
Thou hast warmed me, clothed and fed
    me;
  Listen to my evening prayer.

Let my sins be all forgiven;
  Bless the friends I love so well;
Take us all at last to Heaven,
  Happy there with Thee to dwell!